White Rose MATHS

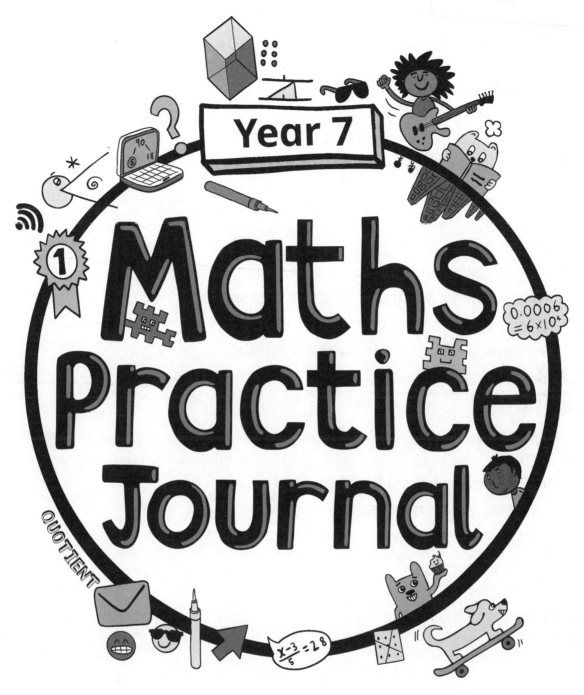

Year 7

Maths Practice Journal

Author: Matthew Ainscough

Series Editor: MK Connolly

OXFORD
UNIVERSITY PRESS

Contents

Autumn term
Block 1 Sequences

In this block, you will explore **sequences** – that's where you find patterns and work out a **rule**. In this sequence, one more circle is added each time.

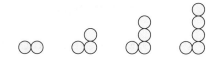

You can also find the rule for sequences of numbers. In this sequence, the rule is add 3 each time.

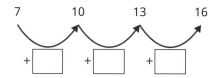

A table of values can be used to represent a sequence. They help to organise the sequence into positions and terms.

In this sequence, the **term** in the second **position** is 8, because there's 8 squares.

The table of values looks like this.

Position	1	2	3
Term	5	8	11

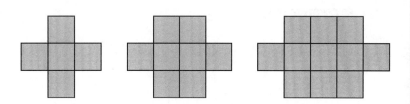

You can also use a **graph** to represent a sequence. The graph shown below represents the sequence of circles. The dots on the graph are in a straight line because the sequence is **linear**.

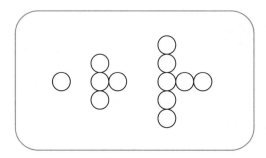

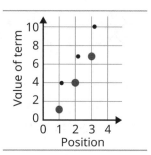

Key vocabulary

sequence   term   position   rule   term-to-term

table   graph   linear   non-linear   increasing   decreasing

Sequences

Date:

Let's remember

1   Work out the area of the rectangle.

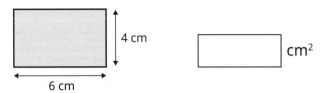

4 cm

6 cm

◻ cm²

2   Work out the difference between 14 and 31 ◻

3   What is 4 more than −3? ◻

4   Work out 4.4 × 100 ◻

Let's practise

1   Describe what is happening to make each new term in the sequence.

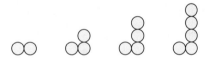

_____

_____

2   Draw the next two terms in the sequence.

3   Draw the next two terms in the sequence.

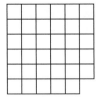      

4 Here is a sequence of patterns.

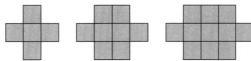

a) Complete the table of values to match the sequence.

Position	1	2	3
Term	5		

b) How many squares will be in the next term of the sequence?

5 A sequence of patterns has been made using straws.

a) How many matchsticks are in each term of this sequence?

          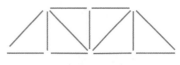

b) How many matchsticks will be in the 5th term?

c) Draw the 5th term to check your answer.

6 Match the sequences to the graphs.

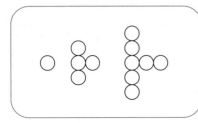   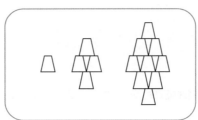   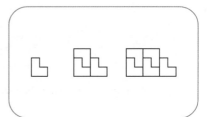

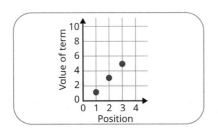   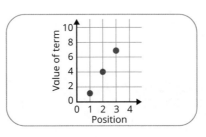   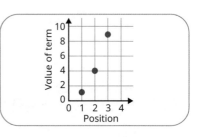

7 Fill in the gaps to describe how each sequence is increasing.

Then decide if the sequence is linear or non-linear. Circle your answers.

a)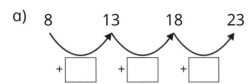

                                                                  Linear   Non-linear

b)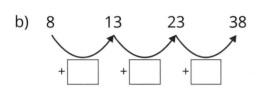

                                                                  Linear   Non-linear

8 Is each sequence linear or non-linear?

a) 10, 20, 30, 40, 50, ... _____

b) 10, 20, 40, 80, 160, ... _____

c) 10, 20, 30, 20, 10, ... _____

d) 10, 20, 28, 34, 38, ... _____

9 The diagrams represent the first two terms of a sequence.

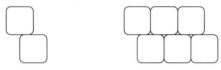

a) Draw the next term in the sequence if the sequence is **linear**.

b) If the sequence is **non-linear**, what could the next term be?

How did you find these questions?

Very easy   1   2   3   4   5   6   7   8   9   10   Very difficult

Sequences

Date:

Let's remember

1 Is the sequence 2, 5, 8, 11, ... linear or non-linear? _____

2 Write $\frac{7}{10}$ as a percentage. ⬚ %

3 List all the factors of 12 _____

4 For every 1 table in a café, there are 4 chairs.

There are 8 tables in the café.

How many chairs are there? ⬚

Let's practise

1 Write the next three terms in these linear sequences.

a) 11, 15, 19, ⬚ , ⬚ , ⬚

b) 146, 180, 214, ⬚ , ⬚ , ⬚

c) 32, 26, 20, ⬚ , ⬚ , ⬚

d) 2.7, 9.9, 17.1, ⬚ , ⬚ , ⬚

2 Write the next three terms in these non-linear sequences.

a) 200, 400, 800, ⬚ , ⬚ , ⬚

b) 100 000, 10 000, 1000, ⬚ , ⬚ , ⬚

c) 4, 5, 4, 5, 4, ⬚ , ⬚ , ⬚

d) 6.9, 6.8, 6.6, ⬚ , ⬚ , ⬚

3 A linear sequence starts with 60 and has a constant difference of 15

a) Write the next four terms if the sequence is increasing.

60   ⬚   ⬚   ⬚   ⬚

b) Write the next four terms if the sequence is decreasing.

60   ⬚   ⬚   ⬚   ⬚

4   Find the missing terms of each increasing linear sequence if the constant difference is 32

a) 160, ☐ , ☐ , ☐ , ☐

b) 128, ☐ , ☐ , ☐ , ☐

c) ☐ , ☐ , ☐ , ☐ , 160

5   Continue each sequence with the rule given:

a) *"add 1 and then multiply by 2"*

5   ☐   ☐   ☐   ☐

b) *"multiply by 2 and then add 1"*

5   ☐   ☐   ☐   ☐

6   a) Match the sequences to the term-to-term rules.

2, 5, 17, 65, 257, ...	Double the previous term each time
5, 10, 5, 10, 5, ...	Halve the previous difference and then add onto the previous term
3, 6, 12, 24, 48, ...	Increase the previous difference by 1 each time
40, 36, 31, 25, 18, ...	Multiply the previous term by 4 then subtract 3
20, 60, 80, 90, 95, ...	

b) Write a term-to-term rule for the sequence that does not match up.

7 Find the missing terms in these linear sequences.

H

a) 100, 220, [ ], [ ], [ ]

b) 100, [ ], 220, [ ], [ ]

c) 100, [ ], [ ], 220, [ ]

d) 100, [ ], [ ], [ ], 220

e) 100, [ ], [ ], [ ], 20

8 The fourth term of an increasing linear sequence is 44 and the constant difference is 8

H

Find the sum of the 1st term and the 8th term.

[ ]

9 The first two terms of a sequence are 4 and 8

a) Write down a term-to-term rule if the sequence is linear.

_____

b) Write down a term-to-term rule if the sequence is non-linear.

_____

10 The 7th term of a decreasing linear sequence is 19

H

The 10th term of the sequence is –2

Find the 1st term of the sequence.

[ ]

How did you find these questions?

Very easy	1	2	3	4	5	6	7	8	9	10	Very difficult

Block 2   Understand & use algebraic notation

In this block, you will use **algebraic notation**. That's when you use letters instead of just numbers.

Bar models can help to understand algebraic notation. This bar model represents $6j$

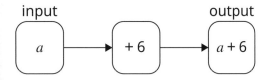

You will be using **function machines** to write **expressions**. This function machine adds 6 to the **input** a to give an **output** $a + 6$

You'll also be using function machines with multiple inputs and outputs. This one multiplies each input by 5

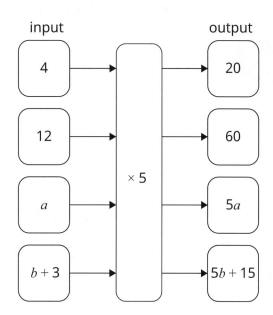

You can use two-step function machines to make more complicated expressions. This one starts with z, which is then divided by 3 to get $\frac{z}{3}$. Then 7 is added to get $\frac{z}{3} + 7$

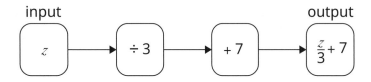

Key vocabulary

bar model   function machine   expression   algebraic notation

input   output   operation   evaluate   increasing   decreasing

Understand & use algebraic notation

Date:

Let's remember

1 Write the next two terms in this non-linear sequence.

3, 6, 12, 24, ☐ , ☐

2 How many counters are needed to make the next term of the sequence?

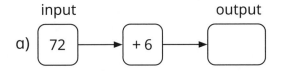 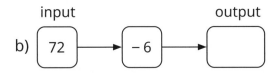

3 Which fraction is greater, $\frac{2}{5}$ or $\frac{2}{3}$? _____

4 Write the value of the 6 in the number 26 078 _____

Let's practise

1 Complete the function machines.

a)
input → 72 → +6 → output ☐

b)
input → 72 → −6 → output ☐

c)
input → 72 → ×6 → output ☐

d)
input → 72 → ÷6 → output ☐

2 Find the input to each function machine if the output is 100

a)
input ☐ → −40 → output 100

b)
input ☐ → +40 → output 100

c)
input ☐ → ×4 → output 100

d)
input ☐ → ÷4 → output 100

3 Complete the function machines.

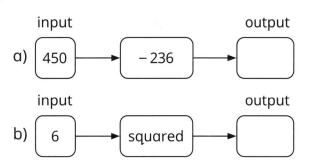
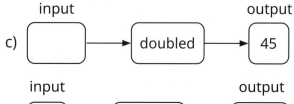
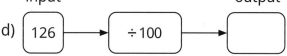

4 Find the output of each function machine if the input is a

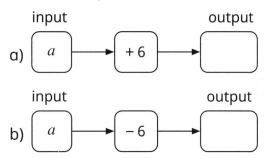
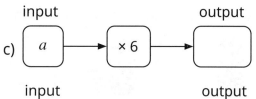
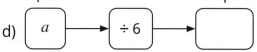

5 Match the expressions to the bar models.

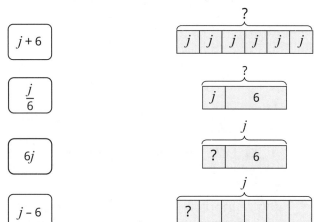

$j + 6$

$\dfrac{j}{6}$

$6j$

$j - 6$

6 Write each expression without the operation.

a) $4 \times t =$ _____   g) $t \times v =$ _____

b) $t \times 4 =$ _____   h) $v \times t =$ _____

c) $t + t + t + t =$ _____   i) $t \times t =$ _____

d) $2 \times 4t =$ _____   j) $7 \times t \times t =$ _____

e) $t \div 4 =$ _____   k) $9 \times t \times 2 =$ _____

f) $4 \div t =$ _____   l) $2t \times 5t =$ _____

7 Write an expression for each statement.

a) 5 multiplied by w _____   c) c doubled _____

b) d multiplied by w _____   d) c halved _____

8   Complete each function machine.

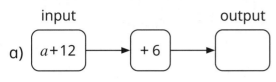

a) input $a+12$ → $+6$ → output

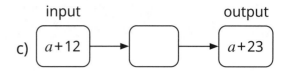

c) input $a+12$ → [ ] → output $a+23$

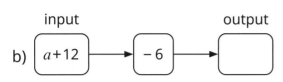

b) input $a+12$ → -6 → output

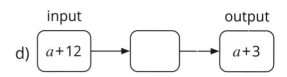

d) input $a+12$ → [ ] → output $a+3$

9   Write two different functions that could complete these function machines.

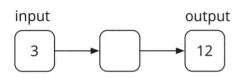

input 3 → [ ] → output 12

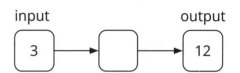

input 3 → [ ] → output 12

10   Complete the function machines.

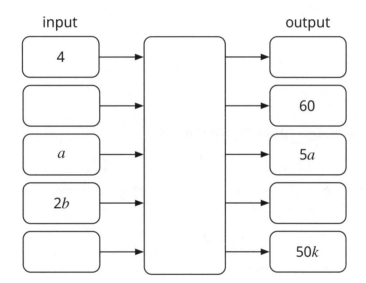

input
4
[ ]
a
$2b$
[ ]

output
[ ]
60
$5a$
[ ]
$50k$

11   Substitute $p = 8$ into each expression.

a) $p + 5 =$ [ ]

b) $p - 5 =$ [ ]

c) $5p =$ [ ]

d) $\dfrac{p}{5} =$ [ ]

e) $50 + p =$ [ ]

f) $50 - p =$ [ ]

g) $p^2 =$ [ ]

h) $\dfrac{50}{p} =$ [ ]

How did you find these questions?

Very easy   1   2   3   4   5   6   7   8   9   10   Very difficult

Understand & use algebraic notation

Date:

Let's remember

1 Find the input of the function machine.

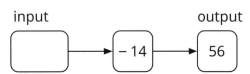

input   output

2 Write the next three terms in the linear sequence.

14.1, 15.2, 16.3, [   ] , [   ] , [   ]

3 Round 2.7 to the nearest integer. [   ]

4 Work out 835 ÷ 5 [   ]

Let's practise

1 Complete these two-step function machines.

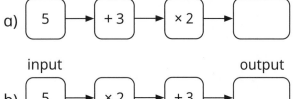

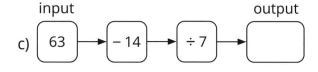

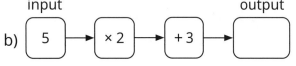

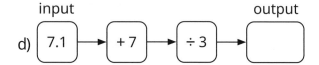

2 Complete these two step-function machines.

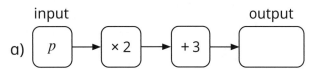

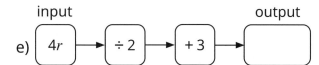

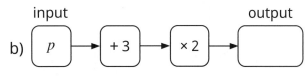

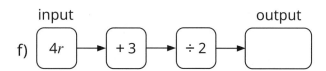

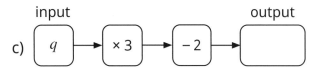

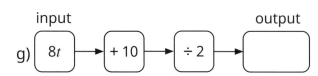

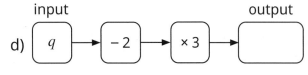

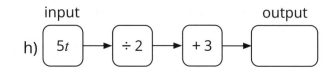

3   Complete these two-step function machines.

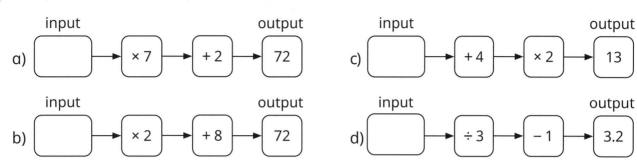

a) input [   ] → ×7 → +2 → 72 output

b) input [   ] → ×2 → +8 → 72 output

c) input [   ] → +4 → ×2 → 13 output

d) input [   ] → ÷3 → −1 → 3.2 output

4   Find the input of each function machine.

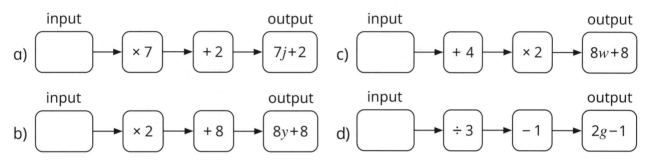

a) input [   ] → ×7 → +2 → $7j+2$ output

b) input [   ] → ×2 → +8 → $8y+8$ output

c) input [   ] → +4 → ×2 → $8w+8$ output

d) input [   ] → ÷3 → −1 → $2g-1$ output

5   Complete these two-step function machines.

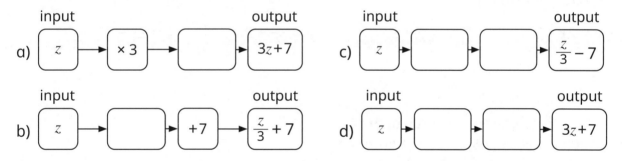

a) input z → ×3 → [   ] → $3z+7$ output

b) input z → [   ] → +7 → $\frac{z}{3}+7$ output

c) input z → [   ] → [   ] → $\frac{z}{3}-7$ output

d) input z → [   ] → [   ] → $3z+7$ output

6   Complete these two-step function machines.

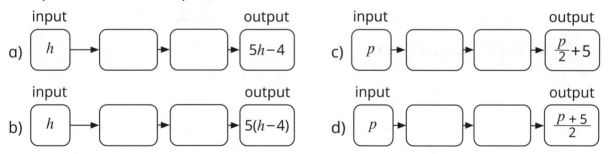

a) input h → [   ] → [   ] → $5h-4$ output

b) input h → [   ] → [   ] → $5(h-4)$ output

c) input p → [   ] → [   ] → $\frac{p}{2}+5$ output

d) input p → [   ] → [   ] → $\frac{p+5}{2}$ output

7   There are n sweets in a bag.

Max has 5 bags of sweets.

He eats 7 sweets from one of the bags.

Write an expression for the number of sweets he has left.

_____

8 Evaluate each expression when $m = 9$

a) $5m + 4 = \boxed{}$

e) $7(m + 1) = \boxed{}$

b) $9z + 9.9 = \boxed{}$

f) $7(10 - m) = \boxed{}$

c) $3 + 4m = \boxed{}$

g) $\frac{m + 7}{4} = \boxed{}$

d) $30 - 2m = \boxed{}$

h) $\frac{m}{3} + 6 = \boxed{}$

9 Find the first five terms of the sequences given by these rules.

a) $\frac{n}{5} + 8$ $\boxed{}$ $\boxed{}$ $\boxed{}$ $\boxed{}$ $\boxed{}$

b) $\frac{n + 8}{5}$ $\boxed{}$ $\boxed{}$ $\boxed{}$ $\boxed{}$ $\boxed{}$

c) $8 - \frac{n}{5}$ $\boxed{}$ $\boxed{}$ $\boxed{}$ $\boxed{}$ $\boxed{}$

10 Which of these equations will produce a **non-linear** graph?

Circle your answers.

$y = 2x + 3$ $y = x^2 + 3$ $y = \frac{x}{2} + 3$ $y = 2x - 3$

11

I predict that the value of the 4th term will be greater in sequence B than in sequence A.

Sequence A: $5n + 8$ Sequence B: $8n - 5$

a) Show that Whitney is wrong.

_____

_____

b) Find the smallest value of n where sequence B is greater than sequence A.

_____

_____

How did you find these questions?

Very easy   1   2   3   4   5   6   7   8   9   10   Very difficult

Block 3 Equality & equivalence

In this block, you'll be exploring **equivalence**. That's where **expressions** are **equal** to each other.

Bar models can help. The fact family for this bar model gives four equivalent statements.

64	
21	33

$$21 + 33 = 64$$
$$33 + 21 = 64$$
$$64 - 21 = 33$$
$$64 - 33 = 21$$

Bar models can also help to find equivalent expressions involving letters. This bar model shows expressions that are equivalent to $4 + 8x$. For example, $4(2x + 1) \equiv 4 + 8x$

$4 + 8x$											
1	1	1	1	x	x	x	x	x	x	x	x
x	x	x	x	x	x	x	x	1	1	1	1
x	x	1	x	x	1	x	x	1	x	x	1
$2x + 1$			$2x + 1$			$2x + 1$			$2x + 1$		

15.1	
8.3	c

Bar models can also help **solve equations**. An equation is where there's an **unknown** value to find. In this equation the unknown value is c: $15.1 - c = 8.3$

The bar model can help to work out that $c = 6.8$

You'll be using tables to organise **terms** into **like terms** and **unlike terms**. Terms are like when they involve the same **powers** of the same letters. If an expression has like terms, you can **simplify** it.

Like terms	Terms	Unlike terms
✔	$3r^2$ and r^2	
	$3r$ and $3r^2$	✔
	r^2 and t^2	✔

Key vocabulary

equivalence equality equation expression bar model fact family

solve like terms unlike terms powers simplify

Equality & equivalence

Date:

Let's remember

1   Write an expression for the output of the function machine.

input   output

k → × 4 → + 5 →

2   Write an expression for p multiplied by q _____

3   Use the diagrams to complete the table.

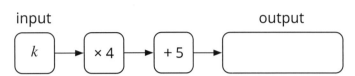

Position	1	2	3
Term			

4   Write $\frac{8}{20}$ in its simplest form. _____

Let's practise

1   Match calculations that are equal.

13 + 5	40 ÷ 4
2 × 5	11 + 7
3 + 3 + 3	√16
0.5 × 8	$\frac{12.5}{5}$
4.7 – 2.2	10 – 1

2   Fill in the missing numbers.

a) 12 + 3 = 10 + ☐

b) 46 + 14 = 70 – ☐

c) 32 – 10 = ☐ – 15

d) 40 ÷ 8 = 1000 – ☐

e) 11 × ☐ = 15 + 7

f) 24 ÷ ☐ = 12 ÷ 4

g) 7.4 + ☐ = 8.5 + 2.3

h) 12 × 5 = 1.2 × ☐

3 Complete each calculation.

a) $987 + 642 = 643 + $ ⬚

b) $1000 - $ ⬚ $ = 999 - 555$

4 Write the fact family for each bar model.

a)
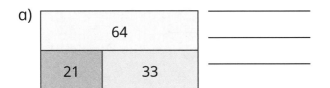
_____
_____
_____
_____

c)
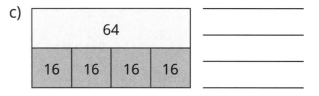
_____
_____
_____
_____

b)
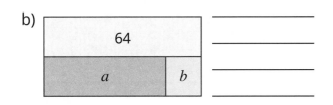
_____
_____
_____

d)
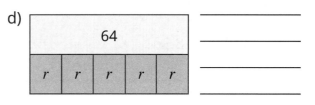
_____
_____
_____

5 Complete the fact family for:

a) $d + 30 = 50$

b) $4 \times g = 17$

_____

_____

_____

_____

_____

_____

6 a) Draw a bar model to show $15.1 - c = 8.3$

b) Solve $15.1 - c = 8.3$ $c = $ ⬚

7 Solve the equations.

a) $y + 145 = 308$ $y = $ ⬚

b) $1001 = t + 12.4$ $t = $ ⬚

c) $24.7 + w = 38.2$ $w = $ ⬚

d) $1.3 = 0.7 + u$ $u = $ ⬚

8 Solve the equations.

a) $j - 145 = 308$

$j =$ ⬚

b) $1001 = k - 12.4$

$k =$ ⬚

c) $24.7 - l = 18.2$

$l =$ ⬚

d) $0.3 = 1.7 - m$

$m =$ ⬚

9 Solve the equations.

a) $10a = 308$

$a =$ ⬚

b) $109.8 = 18.3b$

$b =$ ⬚

c) $\frac{c}{5} = 18$

$c =$ ⬚

d) $0.3 = \frac{d}{5}$

$d =$ ⬚

e) $\frac{35}{e} = 7$

$e =$ ⬚

f) $5 = \frac{65}{f}$

$f =$ ⬚

10 Dora thinks of a number.

She subtracts her number from 126.5 and gets an answer of 99.5

a) Write an equation for this problem.

_____

b) Solve the equation.

Dora's number is ⬚

11 7 less than 12 times a number is 209

Form and solve an equation to work out the number.

_____

_____

How did you find these questions?

Very easy   1   2   3   4   5   6   7   8   9   10   Very difficult

Equality & equivalence

Date:

Let's remember

1 Solve $k + 13 = 21$

$k =$ ☐

13	k
21	

2 Evaluate $10 - 2b$ when $b = 4$

☐

3 Find the missing terms in this linear sequence.

2, 5, ☐, 11, 14

4 Work out $\frac{9}{40}$ of 40 ☐

Let's practise

1 Decide if each of the following terms are like or unlike. Circle your answer.

a) $3r$ and $4r$ like   unlike

b) r and $\frac{1}{3}r$ like   unlike

c) $3r$ and $3b$ like   unlike

d) $3r$ and r like   unlike

e) $3r$ and 3 like   unlike

f) r and $\frac{3}{r}$ like   unlike

g) $3r^2$ and r^2 like   unlike

h) $3r$ and $3r^2$ like   unlike

i) r^2 and t^2 like   unlike

j) rt and tr like   unlike

k) $3rt$ and $4rt$ like   unlike

2   Write the terms in the table so each column contains like terms.

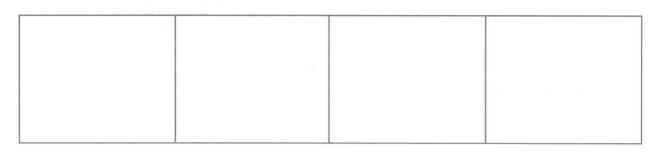

| 4 | 4a | 40a | 40 | 40b | $\frac{1}{4}b$ | 0.4a | –4 |
| $\frac{1}{4}$ | $\frac{1}{4}a$ | ab | 4b | –4b | 4ab | –4ab | $\frac{4ab}{10}$ |

3   Complete each expression so that it is equivalent to $60xy$

a) ☐ $x \times 10y$

b) $15x \times$ ☐ y

c) $15xy +$ ☐

d) ☐ $- 15xy$

e) 20 ☐ $\times 3$

4   Tick the expressions that are equivalent to $4 + 8x$

| $8x = 4$ | $4(2x + 1)$ | $8(x + 2)$ | $2x + 1 + 2x + 1 + 2x + 1 + 2x + 1$ |

5   Simplify each expression by collecting like terms.

a) $m + m + m \equiv$ ☐

b) $3g + 8g \equiv$ ☐

c) $j + 6j + 4j \equiv$ ☐

d) $4r - r \equiv$ ☐

e) $4u - 3u \equiv$ ☐

f) $2t - 5t \equiv$ ☐

g) $-8f + 10f \equiv$ ☐

h) $12d^2 + 8d^2 \equiv$ ☐

i) $16a - 15a - a \equiv$ ☐

j) $3ab + 4ba \equiv$ ☐

6   Complete the grid so that the total of each row and column is $6m$

$-2m$	$8m$	
$2m$		m

7   Annie is simplifying expressions.

$$5a + 5b \equiv 5ab$$

Explain the mistake Annie has made.

_____

_____

8   Simplify each expression by collecting like terms.

a) $5x + 2y + 3x + 8y \equiv$

b) $3z + w + z \equiv$

c) $10t + 14u - 6t - 6u \equiv$

d) $10t + 14u - 6t + 6u \equiv$

e) $10t + 14u - 6u + 10t \equiv$

f) $10t + 14u - 6u - 10t \equiv$

g) $12c^2 - 12c + 2c \equiv$

h) $12c^2 - 12c + 2c - 2c^2 \equiv$

i) $6a - 15a^2 + 10a^2 + 3a^2 + 2a^2 - 6a \equiv$

j) $1 - 4g + 5 + 3g + 2g \equiv$

k) $9q + 7u - 8qu + uq \equiv$

How did you find these questions?

Very easy   1   2   3   4   5   6   7   8   9   10   Very difficult

23

Block 4   Place value & ordering integers & decimals

In this block, you will learn about **place value** for **integers** up to 1 **billion**, as well as place value for **decimals**. Place value charts will be really useful in this block. This one shows 3 406 001

M	HTh	TTh	Th	H	T	O
●● ●	●● ●●		●● ●● ●●			●

You'll also be using **number lines** to help **position** and **compare** integers.
In this number line each **interval** is 30. This means the arrow is pointing to 360

150   270

Place value tables and number lines can be extended to **decimals**.
In this number line, every two intervals is 0.1 so each interval must be 0.05

1.5   1.65   1.75   1.9

1.4   1.6

You'll use data given in tables to work out the range.
In this table, the range of distances is
3920 – 3400 = 520 miles

City	Distance (miles)
New York	3454
Karachi	3920
Abu Dhabi	3400
Toronto	3549

Key vocabulary

place value   billion   integer   interval   round   position   compare

estimate   median   range   power   significant   figure

Place value & ordering

Date:

Let's remember

1. Circle the like terms.

   6p   6k   2p   6

2. $19 + 5 = 3 \times \boxed{}$

3. Complete the function machine.

   input   output

   $\boxed{f}$ → $\boxed{}$ → $\boxed{4f}$

4. There are $\boxed{}$ grams in 1 kilogram.

Let's practise

1. Draw counters in the place value chart to show 3 406 001

M	HTh	TTh	Th	H	T	O

2. State the value of the 4 in each number.

   a) 340 _____

   b) 3040 _____

   c) 430 _____

   d) 3004 _____

   e) 3 400 000 _____

   f) 343 303 030 _____

3   Write each number in figures.

a) Two hundred thousand

b) Twenty-four thousand and twelve

c) Two million, two thousand and eighteen

4   Write each number in words.

a) 35 000   _____

b) 3 050 505   _____

c) 300 000 000   _____

5   Rosie writes 1.5 million in figures.

1.5 0 0 0 0 0 0

a) What mistake has Rosie made?

_____

_____

b) Write 1.5 million in figures. _____

6   Complete the number lines.

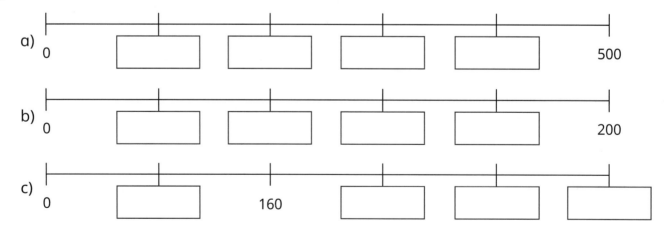

a) 0   500

b) 0   200

c) 0   160

7   What number is the arrow pointing to?

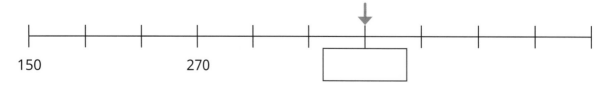

150   270

8   Draw an arrow to show where 100 would go on each of these number lines.

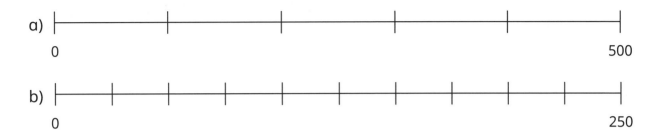

a)

0   500

b)

0   250

9   Estimate the position of 320 on each number line.

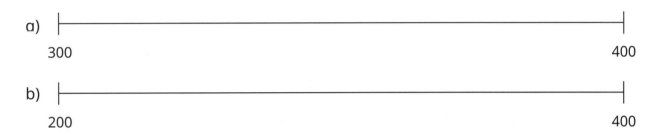

a)

300   400

b)

200   400

10   Complete the table.

Number	Rounded to the nearest 10 000	Rounded to the nearest 1000	Rounded to the nearest 100	Rounded to the nearest 10
8612				
42 745				
210 099				

11   Here are five digits cards.

| 4 | 0 | 5 | 3 | 1 |

Use all the digits cards to make a number that will round to:

a) 34 000 to the nearest 1000   _____

b) 20 000 to the nearest 10 000   _____

c) 50 100 to the nearest 100   _____

How did you find these questions?

Very easy   1   2   3   4   5   6   7   8   9   10   Very difficult

Place value & ordering integers & decimals

Date:

Let's remember

1. Write the number three thousand and forty-five in figures.

2. $10m +$ ☐ $\equiv 12m$

3. Find the first five terms of the sequence with the rule $3n - 1$

   ☐ , ☐ , ☐ , ☐ , ☐

4. A recipe for making 6 bread rolls requires 150 g of flour.

   How much flour is needed to make 12 bread rolls? _____

Let's practise

1. Five numbers are shown in the place value chart.

   Write the numbers in order from greatest to smallest.

TTh	Th	H	T	O
2	5	6	1	2
1	8	9	7	0
1	8	9	6	0
2	4	7	0	9

   Greatest _____

   _____

   _____

   Smallest _____

2. The table shows the distances from London to other cities around the world.

City	New York	Karachi	Abu Dhabi	Toronto
Distance (miles)	3454	3920	3400	3549

   a) Order the cities from closest to furthest distance away from London.

   _____

   _____

   b) Find the range of the distances. ☐ miles

③ Here are the number of letters delivered to the first nine houses on a street.

| 4 | 5 | 0 | 1 | 1 | 4 | 11 | 7 | 1 |

a) Work out the median number of letters delivered.

b) 12 letters are delivered to the 10th house.

Annie says: "The median will increase."

Explain why Annie is wrong.

_____

_____

④ Match the numbers to the place value charts.

1.01

Ones		Tenths	Hundredths
1		0.1	0.01

1.2

Ones		Tenths	Hundredths
1			0.01

1.02

Ones		Tenths	Hundredths
1		0.1	

1.11

Ones		Tenths	Hundredths
1		0.1 0.1	

1.1

Ones		Tenths	Hundredths
1		0.1 0.1	0.01 0.01

⑤ State the value of the 4 in each number.

a) 3.4   _____

b) 3.04   _____

c) 4.3   _____

d) 3.004   _____

e) 0.043   _____

6 Complete the number line.

0 ☐ ☐ ☐ ☐ ☐ ☐ ☐ ☐ ☐ 2

7 What numbers are the arrows pointing to?

1.4   1.6

8 Write < or > to complete the statements.

a) 1708 ◯ 1807

b) 19 006 ◯ 16 009

c) four thousand ◯ seventy-two

d) 999 865 ◯ two million

9 The table shows the heights of Annie, Eva, Filip and Huan.

Name	Annie	Eva	Filip	Huan
Height (cm)	154	145	168	147

a) Complete the statements.

   i) Huan is taller than _____.

   ii) Annie is taller than _____ and _____

   but shorter than _____.

b) Tommy is shorter than Eva but is taller than 140 cm
   How tall could Tommy be? Write down a possible answer. _____

10 These are the number of saves by a goalkeeper in a football team in their first 6 matches.

3   7   1   1   3   6

In the next match the range increases by 1
How many saves could have been made in the 7th match?

Write two possible answers. ☐ and ☐

How did you find these questions?

Very easy   1   2   3   4   5   6   7   8   9   10   Very difficult

Place value & ordering integers & decimals

Date:

Let's remember

1 Circle the greatest number.

23 500   2530   two hundred and fifty three   2 million

2 State the value of the 7 in the number 47 021 _____

3 Solve $13.1 + g = 31.8$ $g =$

4 Work out the value of $12 + 5p$ when $p = 18$

Let's practise

1 Match each number to the place value of its 1st significant figure.

| 341 | 34 | 34.1 | 3.04 | 3401 | 3.4 | 0.34 | 34 000 |

| ones | tenths | tens | hundreds | thousands | ten thousands |

2 Round each number to 1 significant figure.

a) 712

b) 4265

c) 4765

d) 149

e) 149.9

f) 14.99

g) 9.5

h) 90.5

3 Annie rounds 0.057 to 1 significant figure. 0.060

Do you agree with Annie? _____

Explain your answer. _____

31

4 a) Use a calculator to work out $\dfrac{14.1 - 11.6}{\sqrt{20}}$ =

b) Round your answer 1 significant figure.

5 Round each number to 1 significant figure.

a) 4.9

e) 0.499

b) 9.4

f) 0.409

c) 0.94

g) 0.00994

d) 0.094

h) 0.9

6 Write the numbers in the form 10^{n}

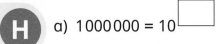

a) $1\,000\,000 = 10^{\square}$

b) $10\,000 = 10^{\square}$

c) $100 = 10^{\square}$

d) $10 = 10^{\square}$

e) $1\,000\,000\,000 = 10^{\square}$

7 Write these powers of 10 as ordinary numbers.

H

a) 10^{3} = _____

b) 10^{5} = _____

c) 10^{7} = _____

d) 10^{10} = _____

8 What is the place value of 1 in each number?

H

a) 10^{4} _____

b) 10^{6} _____

c) 10^{1} _____

9 Write the missing power in each statement.

a) $4000 = 4 \times 1000 = 4 \times 10^{\boxed{}}$

b) $50\,000 = 5 \times 10\,000 = 5 \times 10^{\boxed{}}$

c) $700 = 7 \times 10^{\boxed{}}$

10 Write these as ordinary numbers.

a) $9 \times 10^2 = \boxed{}$ b) $3 \times 10^5 = \boxed{}$ c) $2 \times 10^7 = \boxed{}$

11 Write each number in the form 10^n

a) $0.1 = 10^{\boxed{}}$

b) $0.01 = 10^{\boxed{}}$

c) $0.001 = 10^{\boxed{}}$

d) $0.0000001 = 10^{\boxed{}}$

e) $0.00000000001 = 10^{\boxed{}}$

12 Writing in the missing numbers and powers to complete each statement.

a) $0.0003 = \boxed{} \times 10^{\boxed{}}$

b) $0.06 = \boxed{} \times 10^{\boxed{}}$

c) $0.004 = \boxed{} \times 10^{\boxed{}}$

13 Write these as ordinary numbers.

a) $9 \times 10^{-2} = $ _____

b) $3 \times 10^{-5} = $ _____

c) $2 \times 10^{-7} = $ _____

How did you find these questions?

Very easy   1   2   3   4   5   6   7   8   9   10   Very difficult

Block 5 Fraction, decimal & percentage equivalence

In this block, you'll be exploring the **equivalence** of **fractions**, **decimals** and **percentages**. This follows on from the work you've recently done on decimal place value. This **hundred square** shows 44 hundredths.

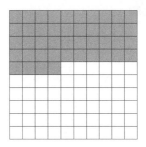

You'll be using number lines for fractions. In this number line, each interval is $\frac{1}{10}$ so the arrow must be pointing at $\frac{7}{10}$. As a decimal that's 0.7

0   1

Bar models can be used to represent fractions, decimals and percentages.

This bar model represents 0.3, or $\frac{3}{10}$ or 30%

You can use your knowledge of **proportion** to construct **pie charts**. In this table, proportions are given as a decimal, a percentage and a fraction. These quantities can be used to complete the pie chart about school dinners.

Type of meal	Proportion
Breaded chicken	0.5
Grilled Fish	20%
Cauliflower cheese	$\frac{3}{10}$

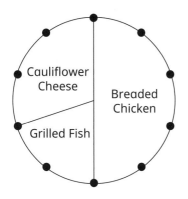

Key vocabulary

fraction   decimal   percentage   equivalent   hundred square   number line

proportion   pie chart   bar model   convert   mean   improper fraction

Fraction, decimal & percentage equivalence

Date:

Let's remember

1 Round 4495 to 1 significant figure.

2 Work out the range of the prices.

£14, £33, £6, £10, £12

3 Solve the equation $1.8 = 12b$

4 Work out $\frac{6}{7}$ of 84

Let's practise

1 Match the numbers to their place value chart and hundred square.

One has been done for you.

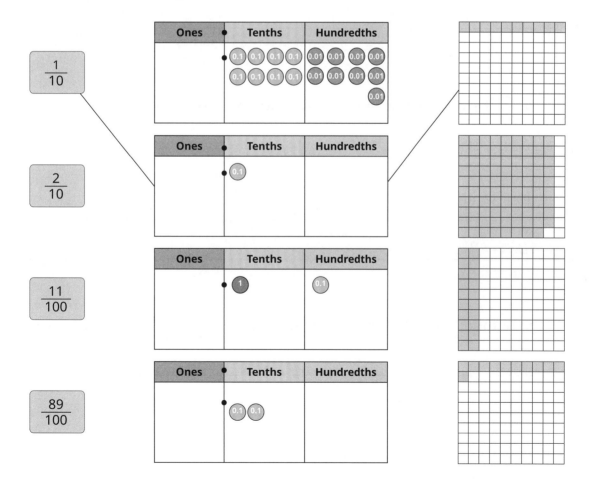

2 Shade the hundred squares to represent the numbers.

a) 4 tenths

b) 4 hundredths

c) 44 hundredths

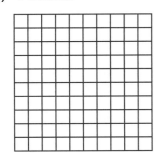 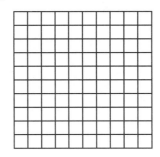 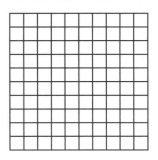

3 What numbers are the arrows pointing to?

a)

b)

c)

4 Draw arrows to show the position of each number on the number line.

One has been done for you.

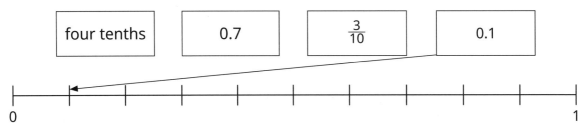

5 Write the number the arrow is pointing to as a fraction and a decimal.

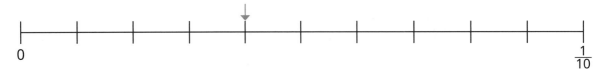

Fraction = [　　]   Decimal = [　　]

6   Write <, > or = to complete the statements.

a) 0.02 ◯ $\frac{2}{10}$

c) 0.21 ◯ $\frac{21}{100}$

b) 70 hundredths ◯ $\frac{7}{10}$

d) 0.49 ◯ $\frac{4}{10}$

7   Complete each part-whole model.

a)
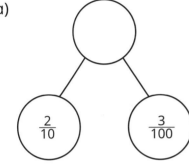

b)
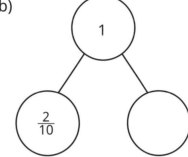

8   Circle the fraction that is closer to 1 whole.

$\frac{4}{5}$ $\frac{3}{4}$

9   Complete the statements.

a) $\frac{600}{1000} = \frac{\boxed{}}{100} = \frac{\boxed{}}{10} = 0.\boxed{}$

b) $0.4 = \frac{\boxed{}}{10} = \frac{\boxed{}}{100} = \frac{\boxed{}}{1000}$

c) $\frac{210}{1000} = \frac{\boxed{}}{100} = 0.\boxed{}$

d) $0.06 = \frac{\boxed{}}{100} = \frac{\boxed{}}{1000}$

How did you find these questions?

Very easy   1   2   3   4   5   6   7   8   9   10   Very difficult

Fraction, decimal & percentage equivalence

Date:

Let's remember

1 Write 0.9 as a fraction.

2 Write 10^3 as an ordinary number.

3 Write fourteen thousand and seventy-six in numerals.

4 The cost of one pint of milk is £0.83
   Work out the cost of 4 pints of milk.

Let's practise

1 Shade the percentages on the hundred squares.

   a) 15%

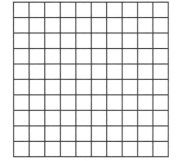

   b) 82%

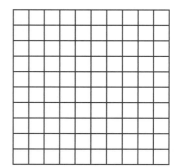

2 Complete the statements.

   a) $\frac{3}{10} = \frac{\boxed{}}{100} = \boxed{}\%$

   b) $\frac{2}{5} = \frac{\boxed{}}{10} = \frac{\boxed{}}{100} = \boxed{}\%$

   c) $\frac{750}{1000} = \frac{\boxed{}}{100} = \boxed{}\%$

38

3 Complete the table for the hundred grid.

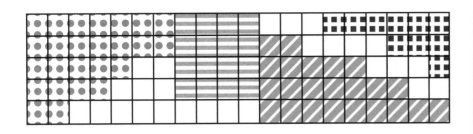

Colour	% shaded
Green	
Yellow	
Blue	
Brown	
White	

4 Tick the diagrams that have 25% shaded.

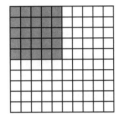 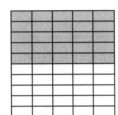 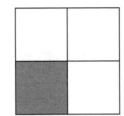 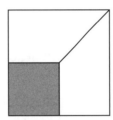 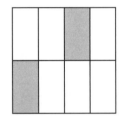

5 What fraction, decimal and percentage of each diagram is shaded?

a)

Fraction ☐   Decimal ☐   Percentage ☐

b)

Fraction ☐   Decimal ☐   Percentage ☐

c)

Fraction ☐   Decimal ☐   Percentage ☐

6 Write < or > to complete the statements

a) 0.25 ◯ $\frac{2}{5}$

b) 0.4 ◯ $\frac{1}{4}$

c) 0.75 ◯ $\frac{3}{4}$

d) 0.6 ◯ $\frac{6}{100}$

7   The pie chart shows the season in which each student of
    a Year 7 class has their birthday.

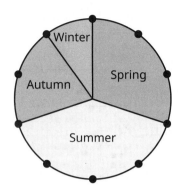

a) What fraction of students have a birthday during winter?

b) What percentage of students have a birthday during Autumn?

c) What proportion of students were born in either Spring or Summer?

Give your answer as a decimal.

8   Tick the diagrams that represent $\frac{1}{5}$ shaded.

9   The table shows results from a survey about school dinners.
    Use the table to complete the pie chart.

Type of meal	Proportion
Breaded chicken	0.5
Grilled Fish	20%
Cauliflower cheese	$\frac{3}{10}$

How did you find these questions?

Very easy   1   2   3   4   5   6   7   8   9   10   Very difficult

40

Fraction, decimal & percentage equivalence

Date:

Let's remember

1 What fraction of the shape is shaded? _____

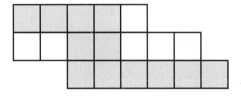

2 Work out $\frac{7}{10}$ – 0.3 [   ]

3 Write the value of the 7 in the number 3.71 _____

4 The mean of three numbers is 8

    What is the total of the three numbers? [   ]

Let's practise

1 Use the diagrams to work out equivalent fractions.

a)

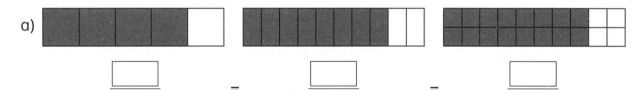

$$\frac{}{} = \frac{}{} = \frac{}{}$$

b)

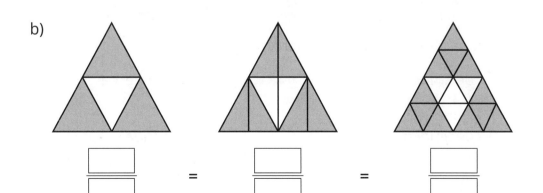

$$\frac{}{} = \frac{}{} = \frac{}{}$$

2 a) Use the bar models to show that $\frac{3}{12} = \frac{1}{4}$

b) Use the bar models to show that $\frac{1}{3} = \frac{5}{15}$

3 Complete the fractions so that they are all equivalent to $\frac{3}{10}$

$$\frac{3}{10} = \frac{6}{\boxed{}} = \frac{9}{\boxed{}} = \frac{12}{\boxed{}} = \frac{24}{\boxed{}} = \frac{\boxed{}}{100}$$

4 Write the fractions as divisions. Use your calculator to work out the answer as a decimal.

a) $\frac{2}{5} = \boxed{} \div \boxed{} = $ _____

c) $\frac{16}{5} = \boxed{} \div \boxed{} = $ _____

b) $\frac{5}{16} = \boxed{} \div \boxed{} = $ _____

d) $\frac{17}{40} = \boxed{} \div \boxed{} = $ _____

5 Write the divisions as fractions.

a) $7 \div 8 = \boxed{}$

b) $14 \div 5 = \boxed{}$

c) $127 \div 128 = \boxed{}$

6 Circle the fractions that are equivalent to $\frac{35}{50}$

Use division on your calculator to help you.

$\frac{45}{60}$ 　　　　　 $\frac{85}{100}$ 　　　　　 $\frac{77}{110}$ 　　　　　 $\frac{294}{420}$ 　　　　　 $\frac{3}{5}$

7 Write each fraction as a decimal and as a percentage.

a) $\frac{12}{40}$ 　　　 decimal = $\boxed{}$ 　　　 percentage = $\boxed{}$

b) $\frac{72}{90}$ 　　　 decimal = $\boxed{}$ 　　　 percentage = $\boxed{}$

c) $\frac{16}{25}$ 　　　 decimal = $\boxed{}$ 　　　 percentage = $\boxed{}$

d) $\frac{27}{125}$ 　　　 decimal = $\boxed{}$ 　　　 percentage = $\boxed{}$

e) $\frac{65}{80}$ 　　　 decimal = $\boxed{}$ 　　　 percentage = $\boxed{}$

8   Use the bar models to convert the improper fractions to mixed numbers.

a) $\frac{11}{4}$ =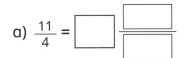

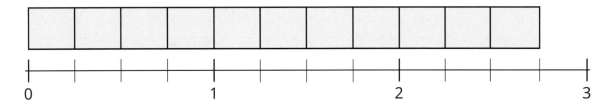

b) $\frac{16}{3}$ =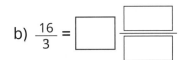

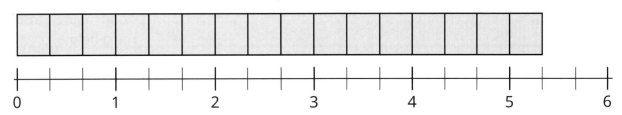

c) $\frac{22}{5}$ =

9   Max and Kim are each thinking of a number.

Their numbers are both greater than $\frac{1}{4}$ but less than $\frac{2}{3}$

Max's number is greater than Kim's.

What number could they each be thinking of?
Write each number as a fraction, a decimal and a percentage.

	Fraction	Decimal	Percentage
Max			
Kim			

How did you find these questions?

Very easy   1   2   3   4   5   6   7   8   9   10   Very difficult

43

Autumn term Self-assessment
Time to reflect

Look back through the work you have done this term. Think about what you enjoyed and what you found easy or hard. Talk about this to your teacher and someone at home.

Try these questions	How do you feel about this topic? Tick the box.
Find the missing terms in this sequence: 15, ☐, ☐, 33, ☐ If you need a reminder, look back at sequences on pages 3–9	☐ I am confident and could teach someone else. ☐ I think I understand but I need practice. ☐ I don't understand and need help.
Write an expression for the output: input: q → × 3 → − 1 → output If you need a reminder, look back at function machines on pages 11–16	☐ I am confident and could teach someone else. ☐ I think I understand but I need practice. ☐ I don't understand and need help.
Find the missing values on this number line. 1.2 ———— 1.4 If you need a reminder, look back at place value on pages 25–33	☐ I am confident and could teach someone else. ☐ I think I understand but I need practice. ☐ I don't understand and need help.
The bar model shows the proportion 0.4 Write this proportion a) as a percentage ☐ b) as a fraction ☐ If you need a reminder, look back at fractions, decimals and percentages on pages 35–43	☐ I am confident and could teach someone else. ☐ I think I understand but I need practice. ☐ I don't understand and need help.

In this block, you will build on methods for **addition** and **subtraction** that you have already learned. **Bar models** will help write down addition and subtraction facts. This one shows that 74 + 19 = 93, and also 93 − 74 = 19

74	19
93	

	3	1	7
+	4	7	4
	7	9	1

You can use **column arithmetic** to calculate additions and subtractions that might be too hard to do using a **mental method.** The answer to this is 791

You'll be applying addition and subtraction methods to work out problems involving the **perimeter** of a shape. In this shape, you need to find that the missing side has length 1.04 m before the lengths can be added together to get a perimeter of 5.44 m.

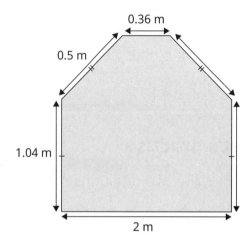

You'll also be using addition and subtraction to solve problems involving other diagrams, such as frequency trees. If you know that 72 of 200 people prefer tennis, and 37 of the 62 adults prefer cricket, then you can create this frequency tree.

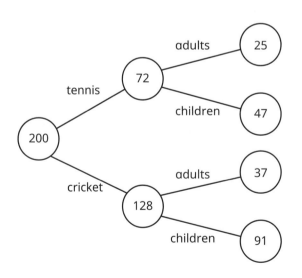

Key vocabulary

addition   subtraction   commutative   total

perimeter   cost   frequency tree   evaluate   expression

Solving problems with addition & subtraction

Date:

Let's remember

1 Write 34% as a decimal.

2 What percentage of the diagram is shaded?

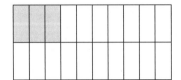

[   ] %

3 Round 32 700 to 1 significant figure.

4 What comes next?

4, 7, 10, [   ]

Let's practise

1 Write two additions and two subtractions shown by this bar model.

74	19
93	

[ ] + [ ] = [ ]

[ ] + [ ] = [ ]

[ ] − [ ] = [ ]

[ ] − [ ] = [ ]

2 a) Draw a bar model to represent 140 + 50 + 26 = 216

   b) Write down a subtraction fact from your bar model.

_____

3 Work out the additions mentally.

a) 247 + 99 = ☐

b) 76 + 398 = ☐

c) 4100 + 1999 = ☐

d) 197 + 321 = ☐

e) 1998 + 1321 = ☐

f) 7605 + 5995 = ☐

4 Work out the subtractions mentally.

a) 247 – 99 = ☐

b) 1000 – 896 = ☐

c) 180 – 54 = ☐

d) 180 – 111 = ☐

e) 360 – 119 = ☐

f) 360 – 314 = ☐

5 Complete the calculations.

a)

	3	1	7
+	4	7	4

b)

	6	3	4
+	4	7	4

c) 1358 + 622

d) 615 + 1403

e) 4009 + 8992

f) 123 + 4567 + 8910

6 Determine which shopping list has the greatest total.

Shopping list A

Shopping list B

Item	Price
Bananas	£1.10
Yoghurt	£0.80
Milk	£1.35
Bread	£2.49

Item	Price
Bananas	£0.90
Yoghurt	£1.40
Milk	£1.55
Bread	£1.80

7 Complete the calculations.

a)

	6	7	0
–	4	3	3

c)

	6	0	0
–	4	3	3

e) 7246 – 6510

b)

	6	0	7
–	4	3	3

d) 7246 – 651

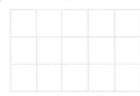

f) 7246 – 6051

8 Complete the calculations.

a) $1.4 + 2.7 =$ ☐

b) $2.7 - 1.4 =$ ☐

c) $1.04 + 2.7 =$ ☐

d) $2.7 - 1.04 =$ ☐

e) $1.04 - 0.27 =$ ☐

f) $2.07 - 1.4 =$ ☐

9 Evaluate each expression when $x = 0.95$, $y = 1.6$ and $z = 0.09$

a) $x + y =$ ☐

b) $x - z =$ ☐

c) $y - z =$ ☐

d) $x + y - z =$ ☐

e) $z + y - x =$ ☐

f) $y - x - z =$ ☐

10 Tommy left his house at 2:15 pm. He returned to the house at 4:02 pm.

Work out how long Tommy was out of the house.

You may use the number line to help you.

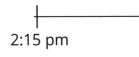

2:15 pm   4:02 pm

☐ hours ☐ minutes

How did you find these questions?

Very easy   1   2   3   4   5   6   7   8   9   10   Very difficult

Solving problems with addition & subtraction

Date:

Let's remember

1. $517 + 488 =$

2. Write $\frac{3}{4}$ as a percentage. %

3. What decimal is the arrow pointing to?

$\frac{1}{2}$　　　　　　　　　　　　　　　1

4. Is the sequence 2, 4, 8, 16, ... linear or non-linear? _____

Let's practise

1. Work out the perimeter of each shape.

a)

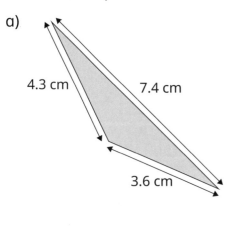

4.3 cm
7.4 cm
3.6 cm

 cm

b)

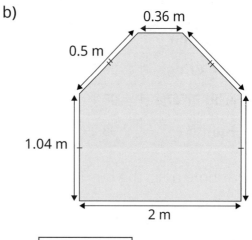

0.36 m
0.5 m
1.04 m
2 m

 m

2. The pentagon has a perimeter of 25 cm.

   Work out the value of q

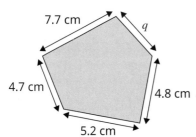

7.7 cm
q
4.7 cm
4.8 cm
5.2 cm

 cm

49

3   Here is the bank statement of a business for December.

Date	Description	Credit (£)	Debit (£)	Balance (£)
1 December	Opening balance			1050.29
2 December	Interest	2.05		1052.34
3 December	Rent		415.32	637.02
10 December	Supplies		38.87	598.15
20 December	Building repairs bill		41.94	556.21
30 December	Income	1865.42		2421.63

a) How much did the rent payment cost?

b) How much did the business pay out in total for the month of December?

4   Here is a bus timetable from Todmorden to Halifax.

Todmorden	07:56	08:14	08:26
Hebden Bridge	08:07	08:25	08:37
Sowerby Bridge	08:19	-	08:49
Halifax	08:29	08:41	08:59

a) What time does the bus arrive in Sowerby Bridge if it leaves Todmorden at 07:56?

b) How many minutes does the 08:14 journey from Todmorden take to get to Halifax?

minutes

5   The table shows the distances (in miles) between three UK towns.

Braintree		
56.2	**Gillingham**	
58.8	73.7	**Luton**

a) Which two towns are the furthest apart? _____ and _____

b) Work out the range of the distances. [   ] miles

6   In a survey, 86 of 200 people prefer rugby to football. 40 of the 72 adults prefer football.

Use this information to complete the frequency tree.

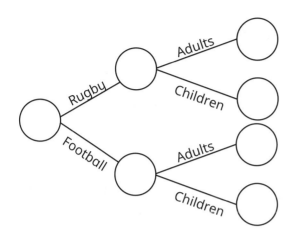

7   The bar chart shows information about how students get to school.

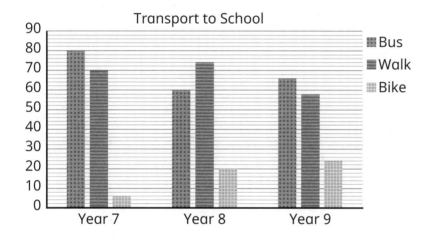

a) How many students bike to school in total?

b) How many more students walk to school in Year 8?

c) Find the total number of students in Year 9

8   The hexagon has a perimeter of 42 cm.

Work out the value for a and b.

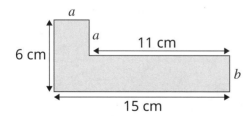

$a =$ ☐ cm

$b =$ ☐ cm

How did you find these questions?

Very easy   1   2   3   4   5   6   7   8   9   10   Very difficult

Block 2 Solving problems with multiplication & division

In this block, you will build on methods for **multiplication** and **division** that you have already learned. **Bar models** will help write down multiplication and division facts. This one shows that 3 × 17 = 51, and also 51 ÷ 3 = 17. Can you see what other facts it shows?

51		
17	17	17

You'll be multiplying and dividing by **powers** of 10, using a **place value chart** to help. For example, 98 divided by 100 equals 0.98. Can you see where to put the digits in this chart?

M	HTh	TTh	Th	H	T	O •	Tth	Hth	Thth
						•			

You can use formal methods to multiply and divide numbers. This shows how to divide 414 by 9, to get the answer 46

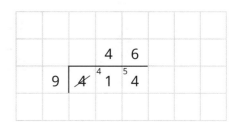

You'll apply your knowledge of multiplying and dividing to solve problems, like the area of this rectangle! Using a formal written method, 81 mm multiplied by 37 mm equals 2997 mm²

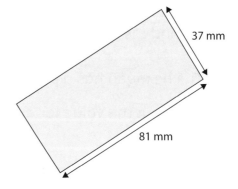

37 mm

81 mm

Key vocabulary

multiplication   division   estimate   factor   multiple   common factor/

multiple   mass   round   significant figure   area   simplify   expression

Solving problems with multiplication & division

Date:

Let's remember

1   A square has a side length of 5 cm.

Work out the perimeter of the square.

[   ] cm

2   Use a mental strategy to work out $713 + 199$ _____

3   Write 0.15 as a fraction in its simplest form.   [   ]

4   Complete the function machine.

input   ouput

j → [   ] → j^2

Let's practise

1

51		
17	17	17

a) Write down two multiplications represented by the bar model.

b) Write down two divisions represented by the bar model.

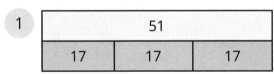

2   Annie says "$42 \div 6$ is 7, this means that $6 \div 42$ is also 7"

Explain why Annie is wrong.

_____

_____

Spring term   Week 3   Small steps 1–6

3 Find all the factors of each number.

   a) 18 _____

   b) 24 _____

   c) 40 _____

   d) 72 _____

4 Find the highest common factor of:

   a) 24 and 40 ▢   b) 40 and 72 ▢   c) 24 and 72 ▢

5 Write down the first 5 multiples of each number.

   a) 15 _____

   b) 20 _____

   c) 12 _____

   d) 18 _____

6 Find the lowest common multiple of:

   a) 15 and 20 ▢   b) 12 and 18 ▢   c) 15 and 18 ▢

7 Complete the calculations.

   Use a place value chart to help you if you need it.

M	HTh	TTh	Th	H	T	O	•	Tth	Hth	Thth

   a) $45 \times 10 =$ ▢   c) $270 \div 10 =$ ▢

      $45 \times 100 =$ ▢ $2700 \div 10 =$ ▢

      $1000 \times 45 =$ ▢ $27 \div 10 =$ ▢

   b) $1.45 \times 10 =$ ▢   d) $98 \div 100 =$ ▢

      $100 \times 1.45 =$ ▢ $98 \div 1000 =$ ▢

      $10000 \times 1.45 =$ ▢ $0.98 \div 10 =$ ▢

8 Solve the equations.

a) $\frac{r}{100} = 7.31$

b) $1462 = 10d$

$r =$ [   ]

$d =$ [   ]

9 Match the calculations that have the same answer.

| 48 × 100 |

| 48 × 1 |

| 48 × 10 |

| 48 × 0.1 |

| 48 × 0.01 |

| 48 ÷ 100 |

| 48 ÷ 10 |

| 48 ÷ 0.1 |

| 48 ÷ 0.01 |

| 48 ÷ 1 |

10 Dexter is making a fruit punch drink for a party.

He mixes together fruit and liquid:

Fruit
- 2.5 kg mixed berries
- 750 g of pineapple slices
- 400 g of grapes

Liquid
- 2.5 litres of orange juice
- 800 ml of cranberry juice
- 1.7 litres of lemonade

a) What is the total mass of **fruit** Dexter uses in the drink?

State your units with your answer.   [   ]

b) What is the total amount of **liquid** Dexter uses in the drink?

State your units with your answer.   [   ]

11 $a = 10\,000b$

Work out the value of b when $a = 720$

[   ]

How did you find these questions?

Very easy   1   2   3   4   5   6   7   8   9   10   Very difficult

55

Solving problems with multiplication & division

Date:

Let's remember

1. Solve $10t = 86$ $t = $

2. $354 + 199 = $

3. Write $\frac{13}{40}$ as a decimal.

4. Complete the function machine.

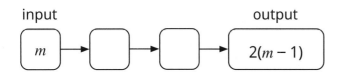

input

output

m → [ ] → [ ] → $2(m - 1)$

Let's practise

1. Use a formal method to work out each multiplication.

   a) 132×3

   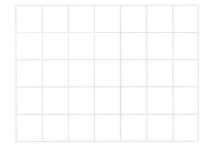

   b) 246×3

   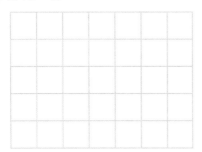

   c) 518×4

   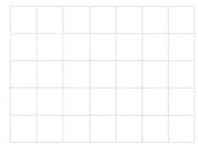

   d) 518×8

   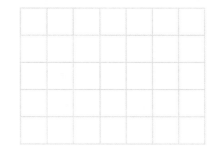

2 Use a formal method to work out each multiplication.

a) 132 × 12

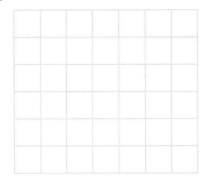

b) 518 × 45

3 Use a formal method to work out each multiplication.

a) 132 × 125

b) 518 × 452

4 Estimate the answers to each multiplication by rounding to one significant figure.

Then work out the calculations.

a) 5.4 × 72

estimate = _____

b) 4.3 × 6.7

estimate = _____

answer = _____

answer = _____

5 Work out the divisions. Give your answers as decimals.

a) 522 ÷ 3

c) 267 ÷ 5

b) 504 ÷ 9

d) 631 ÷ 4

6   Amir is calculating $414 \div 18$

My strategy for dividing by 18 is to divide by 9 and then divide by 2

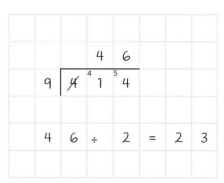

So $414 \div 18 = 23$

Use Amir's strategy to divide $936 \div 18$

_____

_____

_____

7   Work out the divisions. Give your answers as decimals.

a) $52.2 \div 3$

c) $2.67 \div 5$

b) $50.4 \div 9$

d) $0.631 \div 4$

8   Work out the divisions.

a) $273.6 \div 16$

b) $159.75 \div 45$

9   Complete each calculation.

a) $30 - 10 \times 2 =$ ⬚

c) $6 + 4^2 \div 2 =$ ⬚

b) $15 \times \sqrt{9} - 6 =$ ⬚

d) $5 \times 12 \div 3 =$ ⬚

10   Insert brackets into these calculations to make them correct.

a) $15 \div 9 - 4 \times 4 = 12$

b) $4 + 7 \times 2 \div 3 = 6$

How did you find these questions?

Very easy   1   2   3   4   5   6   7   8   9   10   Very difficult

Solving problems with multiplication & division

Date:

Let's remember

1 Multiply 32 by 0.4

2 Convert 5120 ml into litres

3 Work out six hundred and eight plus one thousand, three hundred and eighty-three.

4 13 – ☐ = 30 ÷ 5

Let's practise

1 Work out the area of the parallelogram.

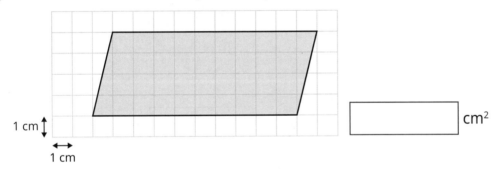

1 cm

1 cm

cm²

2 Work out the area of each rectangle.

a)

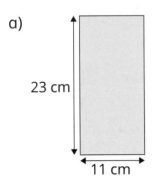

23 cm

11 cm

cm²

b)

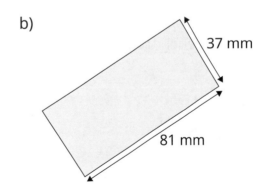

37 mm

81 mm

mm²

3 A rectangle has an area of 180 m²

Find five possible lengths and widths (whole numbers only) and write them in the table.

Length (m)					
Width (m)					

4 Write two different calculations that work out the area of the parallelogram.

Check that they give the same answer.

_____

_____

_____

5 Work out the area of each triangle.

a)

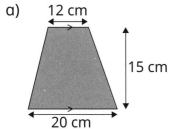

7 mm
24 mm
25 mm

[ ] mm²

b)

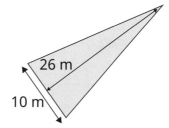

26 m
10 m

[ ] m²

6 Find the area of each trapezium.

H

a)

12 cm
15 cm
20 cm

[ ]

b)

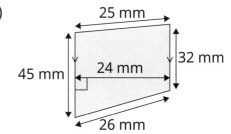

25 mm
45 mm   24 mm   32 mm
26 mm

[ ]

7   The mean of these four cards is 10

Find the value of the unknown digit card.

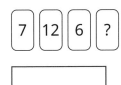

8   Simplify the expressions.

H

a) i) $7x \times 3 =$

ii) $7 \times 3x =$

iii) $x \times 3x =$

iv) $7x \times 3x =$

v) $7x \times 3y =$

vi) $7x \times 3y \times z =$

b) i) $20ab \div 4 =$

ii) $20ab \div 4b =$

iii) $20ab \div ab =$

iv) $20ab \div 4ab =$

v) $20a^2b \div 4ab =$

vi) $20ab^2 \div 4ab =$

9   Write an expression for the area of the triangle.

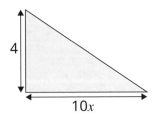

_____

10   What fraction of the square is shaded in?

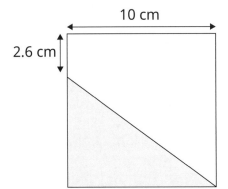

_____

_____

How did you find these questions?

Very easy   1   2   3   4   5   6   7   8   9   10   Very difficult

Block 3   Fractions & percentages of amounts

In this block, you'll build on finding a fraction of an amount that you have already learned, and extending it to percentages of amounts. **Bar models** will help work out fractions of amounts, like $\frac{2}{5}$ of 45. Can you see what the answer is?

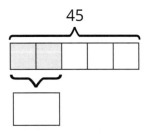

Bar models can also be used to work out the whole amount when you know a fraction of the amount. In this example, 2 of something equals 90. The answer here is 225

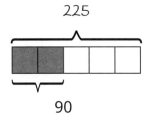

You can also use **number lines** for working out percentages of amounts. This shows that 20% of 135 is 27

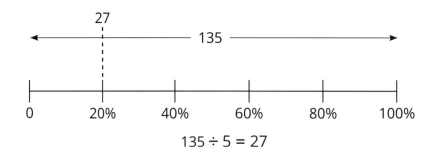

$$135 \div 5 = 27$$

Key vocabulary

fraction   percentage   bar model   value

Fractions & percentages of amounts

Date:

Let's remember

1. The base of a triangle is 8 cm.

   The perpendicular height is 3 cm.

   What is the area of the triangle? ☐ cm²

2. 48.8 ÷ 8 = ☐

3. 3042 − 2092 = ☐

4. Circle the terms that are like $5gh$

   $9hg$　　　$7gh$　　　$5g$　　　$5h$

Let's practise

1. Use the bar models to help you complete the calculations.

   a) $\frac{1}{3}$ of 45 = ☐

   45

   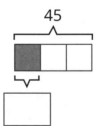

   ☐

   c) $\frac{2}{5}$ of 45 = ☐

   45

   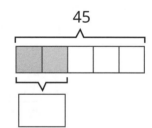

   ☐

   e) $\frac{4}{5}$ of 90 = ☐

   90

   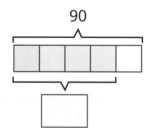

   ☐

   b) $\frac{1}{5}$ of 45 = ☐

   45

   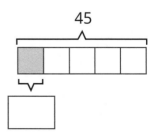

   ☐

   d) $\frac{2}{5}$ of 90 = ☐

   90

   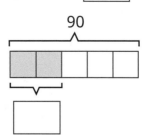

   ☐

   f) $\frac{4}{5}$ of 270 = ☐

   270

   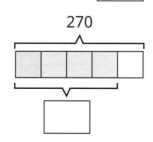

   ☐

2 Complete the calculations.

   a) $\frac{1}{4}$ of 24 = ☐

   c) $\frac{3}{4}$ of 72 = ☐

   b) $\frac{1}{6}$ of 72 = ☐

   d) $\frac{5}{6}$ of 21 = ☐

3 Use the bar model to complete each calculation.

   a) $\frac{1}{3}$ of ☐ = 45

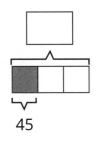

   45

   d) $\frac{2}{5}$ of ☐ = 90

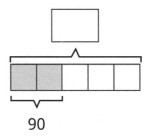

   90

   b) $\frac{1}{5}$ of ☐ = 45

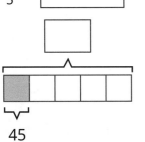

   45

   e) $\frac{4}{5}$ of ☐ = 90

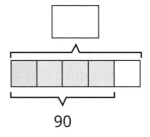

   90

   c) $\frac{2}{5}$ of ☐ = 45

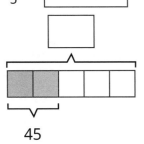

   45

   f) $\frac{4}{5}$ of ☐ = 270

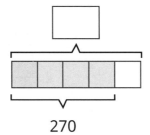

   270

4 Work out the missing numbers.

   a) $\frac{1}{4}$ of ☐ = 20

   c) $\frac{3}{4}$ of ☐ = 36

   b) $\frac{1}{8}$ of ☐ = 4

   d) $\frac{5}{6}$ of ☐ = 60

5 Complete the calculations.

a) 50% of 600 kg = ☐ kg

b) 10% of 440 ml = ☐ ml

c) 25% of £212 = £ ☐

d) 5% of 750 m = ☐ m

e) 20% of 135 cm = ☐ cm

f) 75% of 54 cm = ☐ cm

6 Use a calculator to work out the percentages.

a) 24% of £500 = ☐

b) 78% of £216 = ☐

7 Increase £320 by 7%

Show your working.

_____

_____

8 Find 120% of 30

H

_____

_____

9 Mo's pencil case has blue pens and black pens.

$\frac{2}{7}$ of the pens are black. There 15 blue pens.

How many pens does Mo have in total?

_____

_____

_____

How did you find these questions?

| Very easy | 1 | 2 | 3 | 4 | 5 | 6 | 7 | 8 | 9 | 10 | Very difficult |

Block 4   Operations & equations with directed number

In this block, you'll be working with **directed numbers**. You will see where **positive** and **negative** numbers should go on a **number line**.

−3 and −9 are both negative numbers.

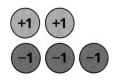

You'll be using **counters** to help with adding and subtracting directed numbers. These counters show that 2 + −3 = −1

You will also be using **bar models** to help with multiplying and dividing directed numbers.
This shows that −6 × 4 = −24

−24			
−6	−6	−6	−6

Bar models can also be used to help solve **equations**. I solved the equation $3h + 1 = 10$ using this bar model.

h	h	h	1
10			

Key vocabulary

positive   negative   directed numbers   bar model   equation   expression

function machine   evaluate   term   geometric sequence   perimeter

Operations & equations with directed number

Date:

Let's remember

1. $\frac{2}{5}$ of £25 = £ ▢

2. The base of a parallelogram is 7 cm.

   The perpendicular height is 3 cm.

   What is the area of the parallelogram? ▢ cm²

3. What is the fourth multiple of 11? ▢

4. Write eighty thousand and twelve in numerals. ▢

Let's practise

1. Write in the missing numbers.

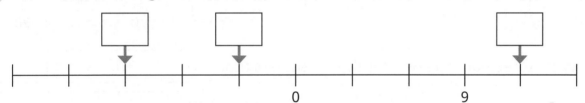

2. What is the total value of each set of counters?

   a)

   b)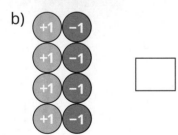

   c)

   d)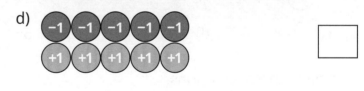

3   The table shows the temperatures of different cities around the world.

City	Temperature (°C)
Anchorage	–20
Berlin	10
Cape Town	23
Detroit	–10
Edinburgh	–1

Order the cities by their temperature from coldest to hottest.

_____

_____

4   Here is part of a number line.

a) Write three numbers greater than C but less than 20 ⬚ , ⬚ , ⬚

b) Write three numbers less than A but greater than –80 ⬚ , ⬚ , ⬚

c) Write three numbers greater than A but less than B. ⬚ , ⬚ , ⬚

5   Write < or > to complete the statements.

a) –7 ◯ 7   c) 5 ◯ –6   e) –9 ◯ 0

b) 3 ◯ –3   d) –6 ◯ –5   f) 56 ◯ –59

6   Complete the calculations.

a) $-2 + 5 =$ ⬚   c) $5 - 2 =$ ⬚   e) $-20 + 50 =$ ⬚   g) $-21 + 50 =$ ⬚

b) $-5 + 2 =$ ⬚   d) $2 - 5 =$ ⬚   f) $20 - 50 =$ ⬚   h) $21 - 50 =$ ⬚

7   Complete the calculations.

a) $4 -$ ⬚ $= -2$ c) $-4 +$ ⬚ $= 2$ e) $-11 -$ ⬚ $= -21$

b) $-4 +$ ⬚ $= -2$ d) $11 -$ ⬚ $= -21$ f) $-11 +$ ⬚ $= 21$

8 Complete the calculations.

a) 10 + −2 = ☐   c) −10 + −2 = ☐   e) −10 + −2.4 = ☐

b) 10 + −20 = ☐   d) −10 + −20 = ☐   f) 10 + −2.4 = ☐

9 a) What is the value of each set of counters?

i)

ii)

iii)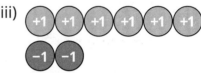

☐   ☐   ☐

b) Tick the set of counters that would help you work out 6 + (−2)

c) Complete the calculation. 6 + (−2) = ☐

10 Complete the calculations.

a) −10 − (−2) = ☐   c) −10 − (−20) = ☐   e) 10 − (−10) = ☐

b) −10 − (−10) = ☐   d) 10 − (−2) = ☐   f) 10 − (−20) = ☐

11 The foundations of a building are 11.4 m below the ground.

The height of the building is 134.9 m.

Calculate the total length between the lowest point of the foundations and the top of the building.

_____

12 Complete the calculations.

a) 24 + 20 = ☐   d) 24 − (−20) = ☐   g) −24 + 20 = ☐

b) 24 + (−20) = ☐   e) −24 + (−20) = ☐   h) −24 − (−20) = ☐

c) 24 − 20 = ☐   f) −24 − 20 = ☐

How did you find these questions?

Very easy   1   2   3   4   5   6   7   8   9   10   Very difficult

69

Operations & equations with directed number

Date:

Let's remember

1   $8 - 12 =$ ⬚

2   $\frac{1}{4}$ of a number is 24

What is the number? ⬚

3   Work out $321 \div 6 =$ ⬚

4   $0.47 = 0.4 +$ ⬚

Let's practise

1   Complete the sequence of multiplications.

a) $3 \times 2 =$ ⬚ $3 \times -1 =$ ⬚   b) $-2 \times 2 =$ ⬚ $-2 \times -1 =$ ⬚

$3 \times 1 =$ ⬚ $3 \times -2 =$ ⬚ $-2 \times 1 =$ ⬚ $-2 \times -2 =$ ⬚

$3 \times 0 =$ ⬚ $-2 \times 3 =$ ⬚ $-2 \times 0 =$ ⬚ $-2 \times -3 =$ ⬚

2   Complete the multiplication grid.

×	6	4	2	0	-2	-4	-6
6							
4							
2							
0							
-2							
-4							
-6							

3   Work out each multiplication.

a) $2 \times -5 =$ ⬚   c) $-6 \times 4 =$ ⬚

b) $-2 \times -5 =$ ⬚   d) $-6 \times -4 =$ ⬚

70

4 Complete the calculations.

a) 2 × 5 × 4 = ☐

b) −2 × 5 × 4 = ☐

c) 2 × −5 × 4 = ☐

d) 2 × 5 × −4 = ☐

e) −2 × −5 × 4 = ☐

f) −2 × 5 × −4 = ☐

g) 2 × −5 × −4 = ☐

h) −2 × −5 × −4 = ☐

5 Use the bar models to help you complete the calculations.

a)

−24			
−6	−6	−6	−6

−6 × ☐ = ☐

4 × ☐ = ☐

−24 ÷ ☐ = ☐

−24 ÷ ☐ = ☐

b)

−40			

−40 ÷ ☐ = ☐

−40 ÷ ☐ = ☐

6 Complete the calculations.

a) −12 ÷ −3 = ☐

b) −12 ÷ 3 = ☐

c) 12 ÷ −3 = ☐

7 Tick the calculations that are equal to −5

| −20 ÷ 4 | | −20 ÷ −4 | | −12.5 ÷ −2.5 | | 12.5 ÷ −2.5 |

8 Use a calculator to work out the calculations.

23^2 = ☐ $−23^2$ = ☐ $(−23)^2$ = ☐

9 Use a calculator to complete the function machines.

a)

input

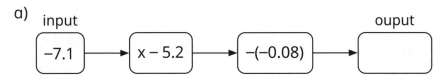

ouput

b)

input

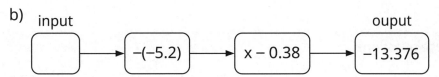

ouput

71

10 Evaluate each expression when $p = -6$

You may use the bar models to help.

a) $4p + 5 = \boxed{}$

b) $11 + 2p = \boxed{}$

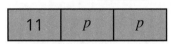

c) $3(p + 4) = \boxed{}$

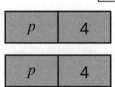

11 Evaluate each expression when $q = -4$

a) $9 - q = \boxed{}$

b) $9 - 2q = \boxed{}$

c) $-9 - q = \boxed{}$

d) $-9 - 2q = \boxed{}$

12 State whether each calculation will be positive or negative.

a) $(-2)^2$ _____

b) $(-2)^3$ _____

c) $(-2)^6$ _____

d) $(-2)^9$ _____

e) $(-2)^{2000}$ _____

f) $(-2)^{4321}$ _____

13 In a geometric sequence, −16 is the fourth term, 32 is the fifth term and −64 is the sixth term.

Work out the first three terms of the sequence.

$\boxed{}$, $\boxed{}$, $\boxed{}$

How did you find these questions?

Very easy   1   2   3   4   5   6   7   8   9   10   Very difficult

Operations & equations with directed number

Date:

Let's remember

1 Work out -6×-10 ⬚

2 ⬚ $+ 12 = 9$

3 The table shows the temperatures at 9 am for each day of the week.

Write the mean temperature of the week.

Day	Mon	Tues	Wed	Thurs	Fri	Sat	Sun
Temp (°C)	13	6	5	5	1	0	2

⬚ °C

4 Write 4×10^3 as an ordinary number. ⬚

Let's practise

1 Evaluate each expression when $p = -3$

a) $2p$ ⬚

b) $2p + 5$ ⬚

c) $-5 + 2p$ ⬚

d) $-5 - 2p$ ⬚

2 Solve the equations.

a) $-4 + a = -11$

$a =$ ⬚

b) $-11 = b + 4$

$b =$ ⬚

c) $-27 = -6c$

$c =$ ⬚

d) $-27 = \dfrac{d}{6}$

$d =$ ⬚

73

③ Annie draws a bar model to solve the equation $3h + 1 = 10$

h	h	h	1
10			

Solve Annie's equation.

$h = \boxed{}$

④ Draw a bar model to represent $25 + 2k = 37$

What is the value of k? $k = \boxed{}$

⑤ Solve the equations.

a) $5z + 27 = 12$

$z = \boxed{}$

b) $12 + 3y = -18$

$y = \boxed{}$

c) $11x + 3 = -19$

$x = \boxed{}$

d) $18 + 9w = 0$

$w = \boxed{}$

e) $4 = 8v + 16$

$v = \boxed{}$

f) $14 = 8u + 16$

$u = \boxed{}$

⑥ Solve the equations.

a) $4p - 8 = 12$

$p = \boxed{}$

b) $4p - 8 = -12$

$p = \boxed{}$

c) $4p - 12 = 8$

$p = \boxed{}$

d) $4p - 12 = -8$

$p = \boxed{}$

7 Complete the calculations.

a) $32 + 6 \div -2 = \boxed{}$

b) $-5 - 3^2 = \boxed{}$

c) $(-5)^2 - 6 \times 4 = \boxed{}$

d) $-9 \div -3 + -2 \times -2 = \boxed{}$

e) $\dfrac{32 + 4}{-2} = \boxed{}$

f) $-(5 - 3)^2 = \boxed{}$

g) $-5^2 - 6 \times 4 = \boxed{}$

h) $-9 \div (-3 + -2 \times -2) = \boxed{}$

8 Solve the equations.

a) $x^2 = 49$ $x = \boxed{}$ and $x = \boxed{}$

b) $x^2 = 16$ $x = \boxed{}$ and $x = \boxed{}$

c) $x^2 = 144$ $x = \boxed{}$ and $x = \boxed{}$

d) $x^2 = 9$ $x = \boxed{}$ and $x = \boxed{}$

e) $x^2 = 256$ $x = \boxed{}$ and $x = \boxed{}$

9 The diagram shows a triangle with side lengths $2k$, $10 - k$ and $14 - 3k$

The perimeter of the triangle is 18 cm.

Calculate the value of k

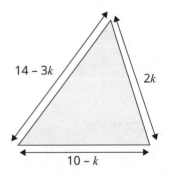

$k = \boxed{}$

10 Work out the calculations.

You could use a calculator to help you.

a) $\left(\boxed{}\right)^4 = 256$

b) $(-2)^{\boxed{}} = -32$

c) $\sqrt[5]{1024} = \boxed{}$

d) $\sqrt[4]{2401} = \boxed{}$

Is there more than one possible solution for any of the questions?

How did you find these questions?

Very easy   1   2   3   4   5   6   7   8   9   10   Very difficult

Block 5 Addition & subtraction of fractions

In this block, you'll build on the work you did on **fractions** earlier in the year. You'll use grids to represent fractions.

This grid represents $\frac{22}{36}$ or $\frac{11}{18}$

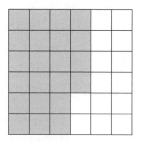

Number lines can be used to convert between **improper fractions** and **mixed numbers**. This one shows that $2\frac{1}{3} = \frac{7}{3}$

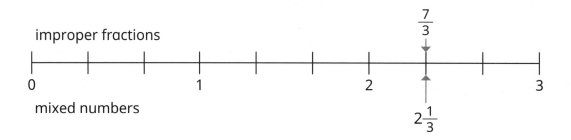

You will use **bar models** to show equivalent fractions. This one shows that $\frac{2}{5} = \frac{4}{10}$

You can also use **bar models** to help with adding and subtracting fractions. To work out $\frac{1}{3} + \frac{1}{4}$ just draw a pair of bar models like this, and then split each of them into 12 equal parts.

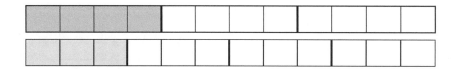

Key vocabulary

fraction   improper fraction   mixed number   equivalent

bar model   calculation   expression   term   unit fraction   mixed fraction

simplest form   evaluate   simplify

Addition & subtraction of fractions

Date:

Let's remember

1 Solve $4g - 10 = -1$ $g =$ ☐

2 $-45 \div -5 =$ ☐

3 Find 20% of 60 $g =$ ☐

4 Which is greater, $\frac{4}{5}$ or $\frac{5}{6}$? _____

Let's practise

1 Draw an arrow to show the position of each fraction on the number line.

$\frac{2}{5}$ $\frac{9}{10}$ $\frac{2}{4}$

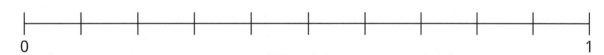

0   1

2 Shade the grids to match the given fractions.

a) $\frac{13}{36}$

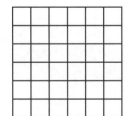

c) $\frac{4}{9}$

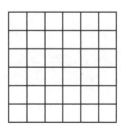

b) $\frac{1}{6}$

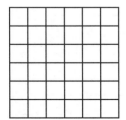

d) $\frac{11}{18}$

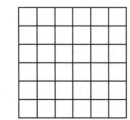

3   Write the number the arrow is pointing at as an improper fraction and a mixed number.

a)

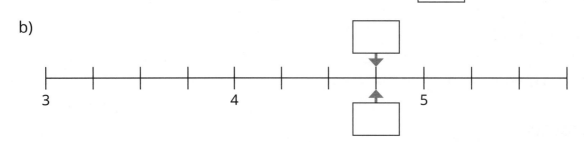

b)

4   Convert the mixed numbers to improper fractions.

a) $3\frac{1}{2} = \dfrac{\boxed{}}{\boxed{}}$

c) $4\frac{3}{5} = \dfrac{\boxed{}}{\boxed{}}$

b) $3\frac{2}{3} = \dfrac{\boxed{}}{\boxed{}}$

d) $2\frac{8}{11} = \dfrac{\boxed{}}{\boxed{}}$

5   Convert the improper fractions to mixed numbers.

a) $\dfrac{7}{4} = \boxed{}\ \dfrac{\boxed{}}{\boxed{}}$

c) $\dfrac{25}{6} = \boxed{}\ \dfrac{\boxed{}}{\boxed{}}$

b) $\dfrac{11}{4} = \boxed{}\ \dfrac{\boxed{}}{\boxed{}}$

d) $\dfrac{80}{9} = \boxed{}\ \dfrac{\boxed{}}{\boxed{}}$

6   a) Rewrite the sequence of improper fractions as a sequence of mixed numbers.

$\dfrac{5}{3}, \dfrac{29}{6}, \dfrac{71}{9}, \dfrac{131}{12}, \dots$ _____

What do you notice?

_____

b) Write the next term in the sequence as an improper fraction. $\dfrac{\boxed{}}{\boxed{}}$

7 Write the fractions as sums of unit fractions.

a) $\frac{2}{5}$ = ☐ + ☐

b) $\frac{2}{11}$ = ☐ + ☐

c) $\frac{3}{8}$ = ☐ + ☐ + ☐

d) $\frac{3}{19}$ = _____

e) $\frac{5}{19}$ = _____

f) $\frac{9}{19}$ = _____

8 Complete each calculation by adding or subtracting unit fractions.

a) $\frac{3}{4} = \frac{1}{4} + \frac{1}{4}$ _____

b) $\frac{2}{7} = \frac{1}{7} + \frac{1}{7} + \frac{1}{7} + \frac{1}{7}$ _____

c) $\frac{3}{3} = \frac{1}{3}$ _____

d) $\frac{0}{10} = \frac{1}{10} + \frac{1}{10} + \frac{1}{10} + \frac{1}{10} +$ _____

9 Work out the calculations.

a) $\frac{2}{7} + \frac{4}{7} =$ ☐

b) $\frac{2}{7} + \frac{5}{7} =$ ☐

c) $\frac{6}{11} - \frac{4}{11} =$ ☐

d) $\frac{6}{11} - \frac{4}{11} - \frac{2}{11} =$ ☐

10 Work out the calculations.

a) $\frac{11}{12} + \frac{2}{5} + \frac{1}{12} + \frac{3}{5} =$ ☐

b) $\frac{10}{13} + \frac{3}{13} - \frac{2}{5} - \frac{3}{5} =$ ☐

How did you find these questions?

Very easy   1   2   3   4   5   6   7   8   9   10   Very difficult

79

Addition & subtraction of fractions

Date:

Let's remember

1. Convert $\frac{11}{4}$ into a mixed fraction.

2. Evaluate $24 - 3 \times -5$

3. Work out $-40 + -52$

4. Shade in more squares so that exactly $\frac{1}{4}$ is shaded.

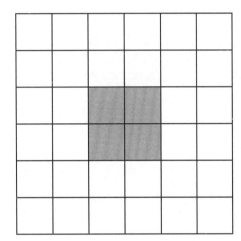

Let's practise

1. Work out the subtractions.

   a) $1 - \frac{1}{6} =$

   b) $1 - \frac{5}{6} =$

   c) $1 - \frac{8}{11} =$

   e) $1 - \frac{6}{13} =$

   f) $1 - \frac{17}{30} =$

   g) $\boxed{} = 1 - \frac{67}{100}$

2. Work out the additions.

   a) $1 + \frac{4}{5} =$

   b) $2 + \frac{4}{5} =$

   c) $6 + \frac{4}{5} =$

   d) $6 + \frac{5}{5} =$

3 Complete the calculations.

You could use a number line or partitioning to help.

a) $3 + \dfrac{2}{5} = 4 - \dfrac{\boxed{}}{5}$

d) $\boxed{} + \dfrac{8}{11} = 2 - \dfrac{\boxed{}}{\boxed{}}$

b) $7 + \dfrac{2}{3} = 8 - \dfrac{\boxed{}}{\boxed{}}$

e) $4 + \dfrac{\boxed{}}{5} = 6 - \dfrac{3}{\boxed{}}$

c) $5 + \dfrac{4}{7} = \boxed{} - \dfrac{\boxed{}}{\boxed{}}$

4 Complete the equivalent fractions.

a) $\dfrac{1}{2} = \dfrac{\boxed{}}{4}$

c) $\dfrac{1}{2} = \dfrac{\boxed{}}{6}$

e) $\dfrac{5}{6} = \dfrac{\boxed{}}{24}$

b) $\dfrac{1}{4} = \dfrac{\boxed{}}{8}$

d) $\dfrac{3}{4} = \dfrac{\boxed{}}{12}$

f) $\dfrac{5}{6} = \dfrac{25}{\boxed{}}$

5 Use the bar models to show equivalent fractions.

a) $\dfrac{2}{5} = \dfrac{4}{10}$

c) $\dfrac{3}{4} = \dfrac{9}{12}$

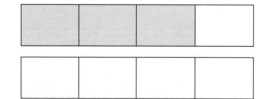

b) $\dfrac{2}{3} = \dfrac{4}{6}$

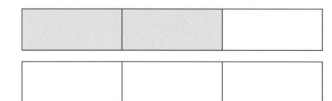

6 Write five fractions that are equivalent to $\dfrac{54}{72}$

7   Ron says that $\frac{14}{42}$ is not equivalent to $\frac{17}{51}$ because 14 and 17 are not

multiples of each other.

Explain why Ron is incorrect.

_____

_____

8   Work out the calculations using equivalent fractions.

Give your answers in their simplest form.

a) $\frac{1}{3} + \frac{1}{12} =$ ☐   d) $\frac{3}{4} + \frac{3}{20} =$ ☐   g) $\frac{4}{15} + \frac{7}{10} =$ ☐

b) $\frac{1}{4} + \frac{1}{12} =$ ☐   e) $\frac{4}{5} - \frac{7}{10} =$ ☐   h) $\frac{4}{9} - \frac{1}{6} =$ ☐

c) $\frac{3}{4} - \frac{1}{12} =$ ☐   f) $\frac{4}{5} - \frac{7}{15} =$ ☐

9   Solve the equation $x - \frac{3}{4} = \frac{1}{12}$

☐

10   Huan is working out $\frac{1}{3} + \frac{1}{4}$ using bar models.

Divide each bar into twelfths and work out the answer to the question.

$\frac{1}{3} + \frac{1}{4} =$ ☐

11   Complete the calculations.

Give your answers in their simplest form.

a) $\frac{1}{3} + \frac{1}{5} =$ ☐   c) $\frac{2}{3} - \frac{1}{5} =$ ☐   e) $\frac{4}{5} - \frac{2}{3} =$ ☐   g) $\frac{4}{5} + \frac{1}{8} =$ ☐

b) $\frac{1}{6} + \frac{1}{5} =$ ☐   d) $\frac{3}{4} + \frac{1}{5} =$ ☐   f) $\frac{4}{5} - \frac{3}{4} =$ ☐   h) $\frac{4}{9} - \frac{3}{8} =$ ☐

How did you find these questions?

Very easy   1   2   3   4   5   6   7   8   9   10   Very difficult

Addition & subtraction of fractions   Date:

Let's remember

1 Find the difference between $\frac{1}{2}$ and $\frac{1}{3}$

_____

2 Complete the calculation

$\frac{1}{5} + \frac{1}{5} + \frac{1}{5} + \frac{1}{5} = \dfrac{\boxed{}}{\boxed{}}$

3 Use a calculator to work out $75 - (-7.5) \times 0.75$ $\boxed{}$

4 Write 0.06 as a percentage. $\boxed{}$

Let's practise

1 Use the fact that $\frac{1}{3} + \frac{1}{2} = \frac{5}{6}$ to work out the additions.

a) $1\frac{1}{3} + \frac{1}{2} = \dfrac{\boxed{}}{\boxed{}}$

b) $2\frac{1}{3} + \frac{1}{2} = \dfrac{\boxed{}}{\boxed{}}$

c) $5\frac{1}{3} + 2\frac{1}{2} = \dfrac{\boxed{}}{\boxed{}}$

d) $17\frac{1}{3} + 11\frac{1}{2} = \dfrac{\boxed{}}{\boxed{}}$

e) $2\frac{1}{3} + 3\frac{1}{2} + 2 = \dfrac{\boxed{}}{\boxed{}}$

f) $7\frac{1}{2} + 3\frac{1}{3} = \dfrac{\boxed{}}{\boxed{}}$

2 Work out the calculations.

a) $1\frac{3}{4} + 3\frac{1}{5} = \dfrac{\boxed{}}{\boxed{}}$

b) $5\frac{3}{4} - 3\frac{1}{5} = \dfrac{\boxed{}}{\boxed{}}$

c) $\frac{1}{2} + 3\frac{4}{5} = \dfrac{\boxed{}}{\boxed{}}$

d) $2\frac{4}{9} - 1\frac{5}{6} = \dfrac{\boxed{}}{\boxed{}}$

3 Work out the additions.

a) $\frac{14}{5} + 2\frac{1}{6} = \dfrac{\boxed{}}{\boxed{}}$

b) $3\frac{5}{8} + \frac{2}{7} = \dfrac{\boxed{}}{\boxed{}}$

4 Substitute the values $q = 6$ and $r = 5$ into each expression and evaluate.

Give your answers as improper fractions.

a) $q + \frac{1}{r} = \boxed{}$

b) $r + \frac{1}{q} = \boxed{}$

c) $r - \frac{r}{q} = \boxed{}$

d) $r - \frac{q}{r} = \boxed{}$

e) $\frac{1}{r} - \frac{1}{q} = \boxed{}$

f) $\frac{q}{r} + \frac{r}{q} = \boxed{}$

5 Solve the equations.

a) $a + \frac{3}{4} - \frac{7}{8} = 0$

$a = \boxed{}$

b) $\frac{3}{4} = b - \frac{2}{3}$

$b = \boxed{}$

c) $c - 1\frac{2}{5} - \frac{7}{8} = \frac{9}{40}$

$c = \boxed{}$

6 Work out the calculations.

Give your answers as decimals.

a) $\frac{7}{10} + 0.1 = \boxed{}$

b) $1 - \frac{6}{10} = \boxed{}$

c) $0.2 + \frac{4}{5} = \boxed{}$

d) $0.6 + \frac{4}{5} = \boxed{}$

e) $\frac{3}{4} - 0.3 = \boxed{}$

f) $0.95 - \frac{1}{2} = \boxed{}$

7 Tick the calculations that are equal to 1

$\frac{1}{4} + 0.55 + \frac{1}{5}$

$\frac{3}{5} + \frac{1}{10} + 0.25$

$\frac{3}{2} - 0.8 + \frac{3}{10}$

$0.25 + \frac{5}{8} + \frac{1}{4} - 0.075$

8 Complete the calculations.

a) $\frac{2}{t} + \frac{3}{t} = \boxed{}$

d) $\frac{8k}{15} - \frac{k}{15} = \boxed{}$

b) $\frac{14}{y} - \frac{3}{y} = \boxed{}$

e) $\frac{m}{n} + \frac{2m}{n} = \boxed{}$

c) $\frac{r}{5} + \frac{2r}{5} = \boxed{}$

f) $\frac{p}{j} + \frac{4p}{j} = \boxed{}$

9 Simplify the expressions.

a) $\frac{1}{f} + \frac{1}{4f} = \frac{\boxed{}}{4f} + \frac{\boxed{}}{4f} = \boxed{}$

b) $\frac{2}{g} - \frac{4}{5g} = \frac{\boxed{}}{\boxed{}} - \frac{\boxed{}}{\boxed{}} = \boxed{}$

10 Simplify the expressions.

a) $\frac{1}{3d} + \frac{1}{4d} = \frac{\boxed{}}{12d} + \frac{\boxed{}}{12d} = \boxed{}$

b) $\frac{2h}{3} - \frac{4h}{9} = \frac{\boxed{}}{\boxed{}} - \frac{\boxed{}}{\boxed{}} = \boxed{}$

How did you find these questions?

Very easy   1   2   3   4   5   6   7   8   9   10   Very difficult

Time to reflect

Look back through the work you have done this term. Think about what you enjoyed and what you found easy or hard. Talk about this to your teacher and someone at home.

Try these questions	How do you feel about this topic? Tick the box.

Work out 74 × 52 using a written method. Show your working clearly.
 	
     T 0
      7 4
   × 5 2
 	
 If you need a reminder, look back at the multiplying and dividing problems on pages 53–61
	☐ I am confident and could teach someone else.
	 ☐ I think I understand but I need practice.
	 ☐ I don't understand and need help.

Use a calculator to work out the output of this function machine. input output -2.4 → $× 3.2$ → $- 0.5$ → (output) If you need a reminder, look back at directed numbers on pages 67–75	☐ I am confident and could teach someone else. ☐ I think I understand but I need practice. ☐ I don't understand and need help.
Using a bar model or otherwise, work out $\frac{2}{3} + \frac{1}{4}$ If you need a reminder, look back at fractions, decimals and percentages on pages 35–43 and addition and subtraction of fractions on pages 77–85	☐ I am confident and could teach someone else. ☐ I think I understand but I need practice. ☐ I don't understand and need help.

Block 1 Constructing, measuring & using geometric notation

In this block, you'll build on your **constructing** and **measuring** skills. You'll be using a **protractor** to construct and measure **angles**. This one shows the angle 40°.

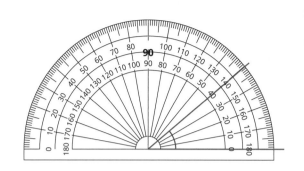

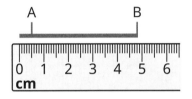

You'll also use a **ruler** to construct and measure **line segments**. This ruler shows that the length of AB is 3.8 cm. Can you see why it's not 4.8 cm?

The points of a **compass** are used to describe directions. If I'm walking towards the east and then I turn 90° anticlockwise, can you see which direction I'm walking in now?

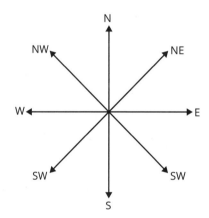

You will learn to recognise types of triangle and quadrilateral. How many of these quadrilaterals can you name?

a)   b)   c)   d)

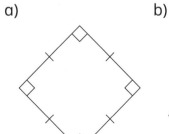 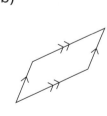 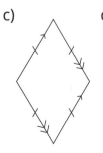 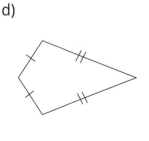

Key vocabulary

line segment   construct   quadrilateral   parallel   perpendicular

acute   obtuse   reflex   integer   equilateral   scalene   isosceles   polygon

quadrilateral   rhombus   proportion   pie chart   frequency table

Constructing, measuring & using geometric notation

Date:

Let's remember

1 Work out $\frac{1}{5}$ + 0.3

2 Work out $\frac{1}{3}$ + $\frac{4}{10}$

3 6 × −2 + −4 × −3 =

4 Find the total of 135, 2040 and 1506

Let's practise

1 Shade in angle PQR in the parallelogram PQRS

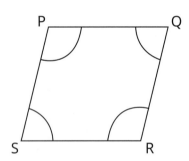

2 a) Draw and label the line segment JK, where JK = 3.9 cm

b) Measure the line segment LM.

3 A walker is facing west. They then turn 90° anticlockwise.
   Which direction are they now facing?

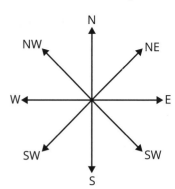

   _____

4 State whether each angle is acute, obtuse or reflex.

   a)

   _____

   c)

   _____

   b)
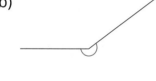

   _____

   d)

   _____

5

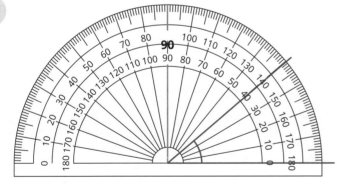

   The angle is 140°

   a) Explain why Mo is incorrect.

   _____

   _____

   b) What is the correct size of the angle? ⬜°

6 Measure the angles in the diagram.

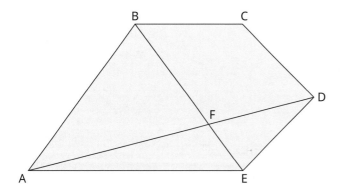

a) EAB _____

b) EAF _____

c) BCD _____

d) DFB _____

7 Draw two angles of 50° using these lines.

8 Draw an angle of 210°

9 Mo thinks of an acute angle that is an integer.

He says "If you triple the size of my angle, it remains acute."

Write the greatest possible angle that Mo could be thinking of. [   ] °

How did you find these questions?

Very easy   1   2   3   4   5   6   7   8   9   10   Very difficult

Constructing, measuring & using geometric notation

Date:

Let's remember

1 Shade in the triangle UXY.

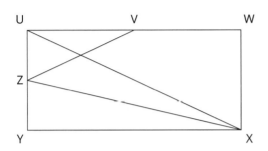

2 $\frac{2}{5} + \frac{3}{10}$

3 Convert $\frac{15}{11}$ to an improper fraction. _____

4 Mo sells a television for £350 making a £70 profit.
Work out how much Mo bought the television for.

Let's practise

1 Tick the lines that are parallel.

a)

c)

e)

b)

d)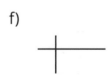

f)

2 Tick the lines that are perpendicular.

a)

c)

e)

b)

d)

f)

3

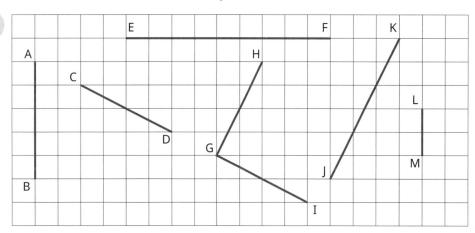

Complete the sentences.

a) LM is parallel to _____

b) CD is perpendicular to _____ and _____

c) EF is _____ to _____ and _____

4 Measure and label the angles and side lengths of the triangles.
Then classify each triangle as equilateral, scalene or isosceles.

a)

_____

c)

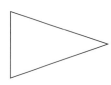

_____

b)

_____

d)

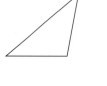

_____

5 Is this statement true or false?
All right-angled triangles are scalene. _____
Explain your answer.

_____

_____

6   Name the quadrilaterals.

a)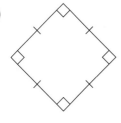

_____

c)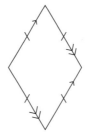

_____

b)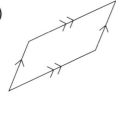

_____

d)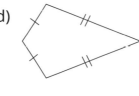

_____

7   Write the mathematical name of the polygon.

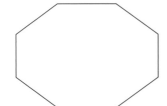

_____

8   Make an accurate construction of the triangle.
Use a pair of compasses.

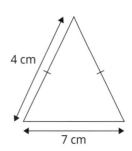

4 cm

7 cm

How did you find these questions?

Very easy   1   2   3   4   5   6   7   8   9   10   Very difficult

Constructing, measuring & using geometric notation

Date:

Let's remember

1   Draw a line that is parallel to AB starting at C.

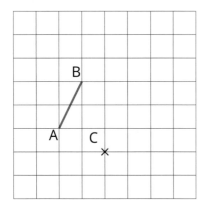

2   Measure the length of FG. Give your answer to the nearest mm.

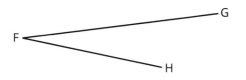

_____

3   $2 - \frac{4}{5} =$ ⬜

4   $0.76 \div 100 =$ ⬜

Let's practise

1   Make an accurate drawing of the triangle.

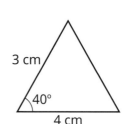

2 Make an accurate drawing of the triangle.

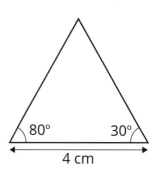

3 a) Make an accurate drawing of the rhombus.

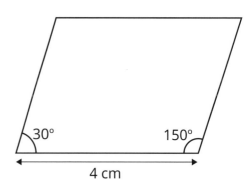

   b) Draw the diagonals of the rhombus that you have drawn, and measure the
       length of each diagonal. Label the diagram with your measurements.

4 The pie charts show the proportions of oat, soya, almond and coconut milk sold in
   two different supermarkets.

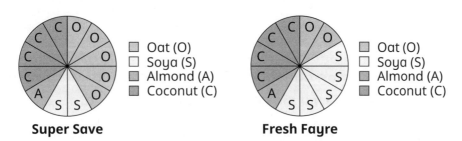

   Decide if each statement is true or false or whether there is not enough information.

   a) Fresh Fayre sold more soya milk than oat, coconut or almond milk.

       _____

   b) Each supermarket sold the same amount of milk.

       _____

   c) Super Save sold twice as much oat milk than soya milk.

       _____

   d) Each supermarket sold the same proportion of coconut milk.

       _____

5   The pie chart shows the proportion of blue (B), red
(R) and green (G) pens in a pencil case.

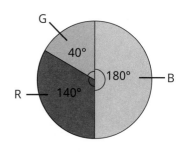

a) What fraction of the pens are green?

b) There are 9 blue pens in the pencil case.

How many pens are in the pencil case in total?

c) How many red pens are there?

6   The pie chart shows what device 180 people watched a live sporting event on.
The pie chart is drawn accurately.

Fill in the frequency table to show how many people used each device.

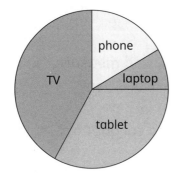

Device	Frequency
phone	
laptop	
tablet	
TV	

7   The table shows information about how far students in Year 7 travel to school.
Complete the table and draw a pie chart to represent the data.

Distance from school	1 mile or less	2 miles or less	3 miles or less	More than 3 miles
Frequency	45	62	58	15
Angle of sector				

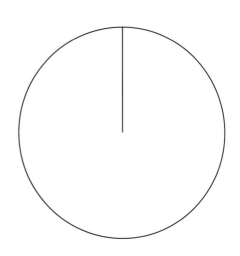

How did you find these questions?

Very easy   1   2   3   4   5   6   7   8   9   10   Very difficult

Block 2 Developing geometric reasoning

In this block, you'll build on your recent work with **angles** to learn about angles in lines and shapes. You can show angles in different ways, like in this diagram. Can you see why x is 287°?

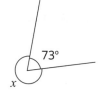

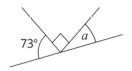

You'll be looking at angles on a **straight line**. This picture shows an angle of 73°, a **right angle** and an unknown angle a that you have to find. Problems like this should be solved by calculation, not measuring.

You'll be solving problems with angles in **triangles** and **quadrilaterals**. In this one, you can use the algebra that you've learned to find the unknown value k

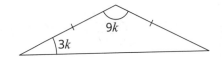

You'll also be looking at angles in **polygons**. This one **is regular** because all the sides are the same length. Can you name this polygon?

Key vocabulary

quadrilateral   polygon   regular   parallel   adjacent   vertically opposite

obtuse   concave   interior   alternate   corresponding   expression

Developing geometric reasoning

Date:

Let's remember

1 A pie chart is split into 4 equal sectors. What is the angle in each sector? ⬚ °

2 What type of triangle is shown?

_____

3 Work out $1\frac{2}{3} + 2\frac{2}{5} =$ ⬚

4 Work out $0.2 \times 0.4 =$ ⬚

Let's practise

1 Find the size of angle x in each diagram.

a)

$x =$ ⬚

c) 315°
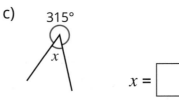
$x =$ ⬚

b) 200°
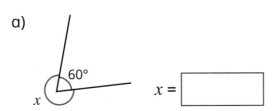
$x =$ ⬚

d)
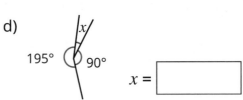
$x =$ ⬚

2 Three regular hexagons meet at a point.
Find the size of angle h

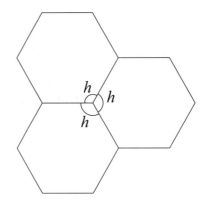

$h =$ ⬚

3 Form and solve an equation to find the size of angle w

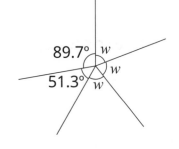

$w =$ ⬚

4 Two angles, *a* and *b*, are adjacent on a straight line.

a) What is the total of the two angles?

b) Complete the sentence.
   Adjacent angles on a straight line _____

5 Work out the unknown angles.

a)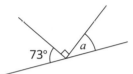

$a =$

c)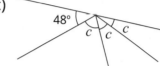

$c =$

b)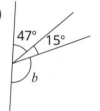

$b =$

d)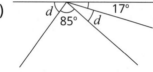

$d =$

6 a) Write the size of the given angles.

PQS =

RQT =

TQS =

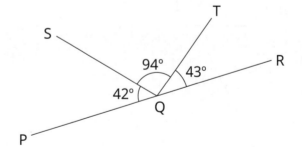

b) Is PQR a straight line? _____
   Explain your answer.

_____

_____

7 Work out the value of y

a)

$y =$ ☐

b)

$y =$ ☐

8 Tick the pairs of angles that are vertically opposite.

a)

b)

c)

d)

e)

9 Work out the unknown angles.

a)

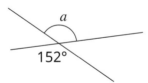

$a =$ ☐

c)

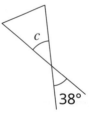

$c =$ ☐

b)

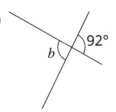

$b =$ ☐

d)

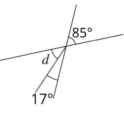

$d =$ ☐

How did you find these questions?

Very easy   1   2   3   4   5   6   7   8   9   10   Very difficult

Developing geometric reasoning

Date:

Let's remember

(1) Find the size of angle p. ⬚ °

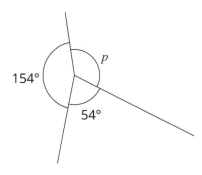

(2) What fraction of the pie chart is yellow (Y)?

⬚

(3) Is the angle acute, obtuse or reflex? _____

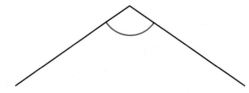

(4) Simplify the expression $3d \times 6f$ _____

Let's practise

(1) Work out the size of the unknown angle.

$p =$ ⬚

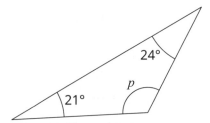

(2) a) Two of the angles in a triangle are 62° and 14°

What is the size of the third angle? ⬚

b) Two of the angles in a different triangle are 46° each.
Tommy says the third angle is obtuse.
Show that Tommy is wrong.

_____

_____

3 Work out the sizes of the unknown angles.

a)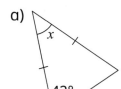

$x =$ [   ]

c)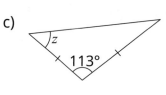

$z =$ [   ]

b)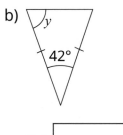

$y =$ [   ]

d)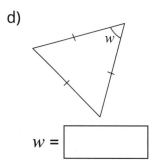

$w =$ [   ]

4 Work out the value of k

$k =$ [   ]

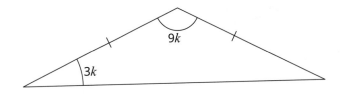

5 Work out the unknown angles.

a)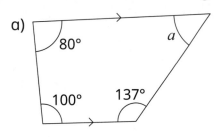

$a =$ [   ]

b)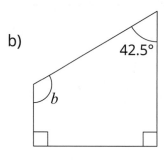

$b =$ [   ]

6 Work out the unknown angles.

a)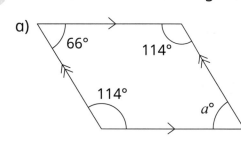

$a =$ [   ]

b)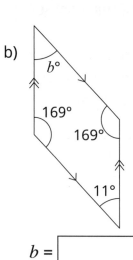

$b =$ [   ]

7   Two identical isosceles triangles are joined to
    form a concave kite.

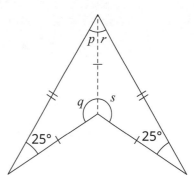

Work out the size of the unknown angles.

$p =$ ☐ $q =$ ☐

$r =$ ☐ $s =$ ☐

8   Work out the size of the unknown angles.

a)

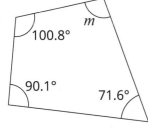
100.8° m
90.1°
71.6°

$m =$ ☐

c)

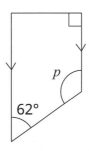
p
62°

$p =$ ☐

b)

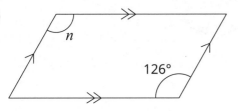
n
126°

$n =$ ☐

d)

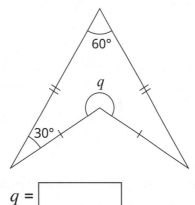
60°
q
30°

$q =$ ☐

9   a) Work out the unknown angles.

$a =$ ☐ $c =$ ☐

$b =$ ☐ $d =$ ☐

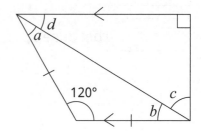
d
a
120°
c
b

b) Complete the calculation.

$a + b + c + d =$ ☐

How did you find these questions?

Very easy   1   2   3   4   5   6   7   8   9   10   Very difficult

Developing geometric reasoning

Date:

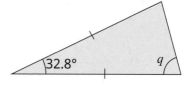

Let's remember

1 Find the size of angle q [ ] °

2 Find the size of angle a [ ] °

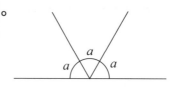

3 Write the mathematical of the shape.

_____

4 Calculate 32% of 32 kg. [ ] kg

Let's practise

1 Work out the size of the unknown angles.
Give a reason for each answer.

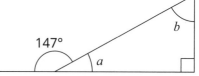

$a =$ [ ] because _____

$b =$ [ ] because _____

2 Work out the size of the unknown angles.
Give a reason for each stage of your working.

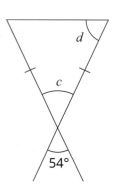

$c =$ [ ] because _____

$d =$ [ ] because _____

3 Work out the sizes of the unknown angles.

a)

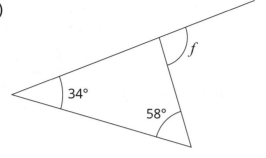

$f =$ ☐

b)

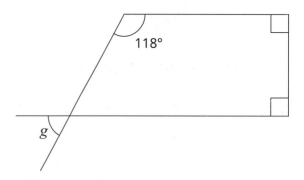

$g =$ ☐

4 Work out the sizes of the unknown angles.

a)

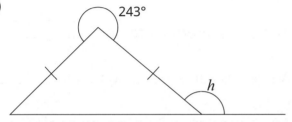

$h =$ ☐

b)

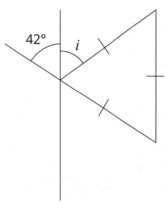

$i =$ ☐

5 Work out the sizes of the unknown angles.

a)

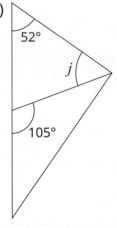

$j =$ ☐

b)

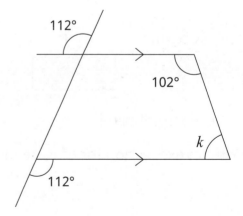

$k =$ ☐

6 Complete each statement about the regular polygon.

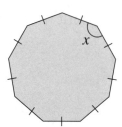

number of sides = ◻

sum of interior angles = ◻

sum of interior angles ÷ number of sides = size of interior angle

◻ ÷ ◻ = ◻

x = ◻

7 Complete the sentences.

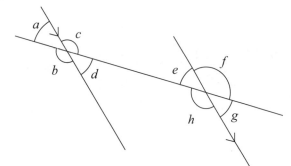

Angle a is vertically opposite angle _____

Angle a is corresponding to angle _____

Angle h is alternate to angle _____

Angle h is corresponding to angle _____

Angle h is vertically opposite angle _____

8 Work out the size of angle x

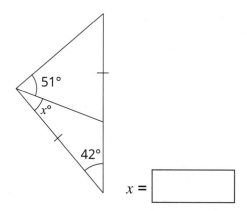

x = ◻

9 ABD is a straight line.

Write an expression for the size of angle CBD.

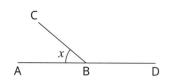

How did you find these questions?

Very easy   1   2   3   4   5   6   7   8   9   10   Very difficult

Summer term

Block 3 Developing number sense

In this block, you will build on your **mental strategies** for working with number. You'll use **mental methods** to solve problems involving **arithmetic**, like this one where the area of a rectangle needs to be worked out.

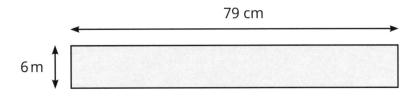

79 cm

6 m

Mental methods will also be used to solve problems that involve money.

There is a $\frac{1}{3}$ **discount** on these two items in a sale. Can you work out what their sale prices are?

£150

£99

You will use **factors** to work out **multiplication** and **division** problems. Can you follow my method to work out 720 ÷ 24?

$720 \div 24$
$720 = 72 \cdot 10$
$72 \div 24 = 3$
$3 \cdot 10 = 30$
so $720 \div 24 = 30$

$32 \cdot 45 = 1440$
$3.2 \cdot 4.5 = 14.4$
$144 \div 3.2 = 45$

Related facts can be used to solve problems involving multiplication and division. If you know that 32 × 45 = 1440 then you can work out lots of other calculations.

Key vocabulary

mental strategies   mental methods   arithmetic

discount   factors   related facts   area   estimate   expression

Developing number sense

Date:

Let's remember

1 Find the size of angle k [ ] °

2 Find the size of angle c

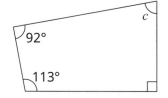

[ ] °

3 120 students brought a fruit snack to school. How many students brought an apple?

[ ]

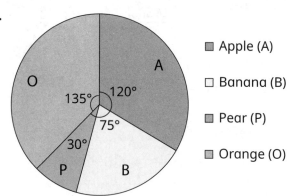

■ Apple (A)

□ Banana (B)

■ Pear (P)

□ Orange (O)

4 11 − (−4) = [ ]

Let's practise

1 Work out the additions mentally.

a) 200 + 150 = [ ]

b) 240 + 160 = [ ]

c) 330 + 410 = [ ]

d) 470 + 330 = [ ]

e) 580 + 290 = [ ]

f) 290 + 490 = [ ]

2 Work out the additions mentally.

a) 35 + 99 = ☐   d) 213 + 98 = ☐

b) 99 + 67 = ☐   e) 97 + 299 = ☐

c) 124 + 99 = ☐   f) 198 + 490 = ☐

3 Work out the subtractions mentally.

a) 86 − 14 = ☐   d) 241 − 99 = ☐

b) 470 − 140 = ☐   e) 7 − 15 = ☐

c) 63 − 39 = ☐   f) 1000 − 491 = ☐

4 Use a mental method to work out the area of the rectangle.

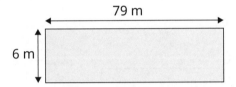

79 m

6 m

☐ m²

5 Use mental methods to work out the divisions.

a) 270 ÷ 3 = ☐   d) 738 ÷ 2 = ☐

b) 720 ÷ 12 = ☐   e) 216 ÷ 3 = ☐

c) 4900 ÷ 7 = ☐   f) 480 ÷ 5 = ☐

6 Ron is working out 340 ÷ 20

What mistake has Ron made? What is the correct answer?

I know that
10 × 2 = 20 so I did
340 ÷ 10 = 34 and then
34 × 2 = 68

_____

_____

7 Work out the calculations in your head.

a) 0.4 + 0.3 = ☐   d) 2.3 + 1.6 = ☐

b) 0.4 + 0.6 = ☐   e) 12.7 − 1.3 = ☐

c) 0.6 − 0.4 = ☐   f) 5 − 0.6 = ☐

8   Lemonade costs 99p per bottle.

Use a mental method to work out the cost of 6 bottles of lemonade.

_____

9   Use mental methods to work out the divisions.

a) $2.7 \div 3 =$ 〔　　　〕

d) $0.632 \div 2 =$ 〔　　　〕

b) $4.8 \div 12 =$ 〔　　　〕

e) $2.16 \div 3 =$ 〔　　　〕

c) $4.9 \div 7 =$ 〔　　　〕

f) $4.8 \div 5 =$ 〔　　　〕

10   A pack of 50 seeds costs £2.50
Use a mental method to work out the cost of one seed.

〔　　　　　〕

11   Work out the amounts mentally.

a) $\frac{1}{4}$ of 32 = 〔　　　〕

d) $\frac{3}{4}$ of 32 = 〔　　　〕

b) $\frac{1}{5}$ of £55 = 〔　　　〕

e) $\frac{4}{5}$ of 55 = 〔　　　〕

c) $\frac{1}{6}$ of 3000 kg = 〔　　　〕

f) $\frac{5}{6}$ of 3000 kg = 〔　　　〕

12   In a sale, there is $\frac{1}{3}$ off the cost of all goods.

 £450    £510

In your head, work out the cost of each item in the sale.

The dishwasher is £ 〔　　　　〕 in the sale.

The washing machine is £ 〔　　　　〕 in the sale.

13   Work out $\frac{1}{5} + \frac{1}{2}$ in your head. 〔　　　〕

How did you find these questions?

Very easy   1   2   3   4   5   6   7   8   9   10   Very difficult

Developing number sense

Date:

Let's remember

1. $412 - 98 = \boxed{}$

2. What is the sum of the interior angles in a triangle? $\boxed{}$ °

3. What do adjacent angles on a straight line sum to? $\boxed{}$ °

4. Evaluate $-9j + 7$ when $j = -2$ $\boxed{}$

Let's practise

1. Here are three methods to work out 15×8

Multiply 15 by 10 then take away 2 lots of 15	Multiply 15 by 2 then by 2 again and then by 2 again	Multiply 10 by 8 and 5 by 8 and then add the results together

   Use your preferred method to work out 15×8 $\boxed{}$

2. Tick the calculations that give the same answer as 30×12

$2 \times 2 \times 2 \times 3 \times 3 \times 5$	60×60	$5 \times 6 \times 6 \times 2$	$30 \times 10 \times 2$

3. Work out these divisions mentally.

   You may use factors to help you.

   a) $360 \div 8 = \boxed{}$

   b) $360 \div 12 = \boxed{}$

   c) $360 \div 24 = \boxed{}$

4   Estimate the answer to each calculation.

   a) 1997 + 1001 ⬚   c) 98 × 8 ⬚

   b) 2.1 × 4.9 ⬚   d) 398 ÷ 41 ⬚

5   Rosie wants to buy these three items.

£1.78   £2.09   £4.99

   Use estimation to decide if Rosie can buy all three items with a £10 note.

   _____

6   Estimate the answer to each calculation.

   a) $\frac{1}{5}$ of £101 ⬚

   b) 25% of 35 kg ⬚

   c) 0.5 × 49 ⬚

7   Use the fact that 27 × 14 = 378 to work out

   a) 270 × 14 = ⬚   e) 27 × 28 = ⬚

   b) 27 × 1.4 = ⬚   f) 27 × 7 = ⬚

   c) 140 × 27 = ⬚   g) 378 ÷ 14 = ⬚

   d) 2.7 × 1.4 = ⬚   h) 3780 ÷ 270 = ⬚

8   Use Annie's fact to work out the calculations.

   a) 179 + 213 = ⬚   178 + 213 = 391

   b) 211 + 178 = ⬚

   c) 390 – 212 = ⬚

9   Tick any calculations that will give the same as answer as 23×32

| 230×32 | | 32×23 | | 2.3×3.2 |

| 2.3×320 | | 320×230 | | 230×3.2 |

10   Dexter works out $2003 - 997$

```
          9  9
    ¹2  ¹0̷  ¹0̷  ¹3
 -     9  9  7
    1  0  0  6
```

Explain a quicker way that Dexter could have done this mentally.

_____

_____

11   Use the fact that $m + n = 6$ to work out the value of each expression.

a) $2m + 2n =$ ☐   d) $\frac{1}{3}(m + n) =$ ☐

b) $4n + 4m =$ ☐   e) $m + n + 4 =$ ☐

c) $9(m + n) =$ ☐   f) $m - 1 + n =$ ☐

12   $u + v = 4$

Use this information to write expressions that would give these values.

a) $8 =$ _____   b) $20 =$ _____   c) $0.4 =$ _____

How did you find these questions?

Very easy   1   2   3   4   5   6   7   8   9   10   Very difficult

Block 4 Sets & probability

In this block, you will learn about **sets** and **probability**. **Venn diagrams** can be used to describe sets, like this one:

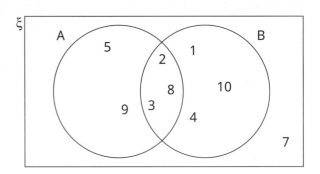

There'll be lots of new **vocabulary** and **notation** to learn for sets, like here for example. That funny squiggly symbol at the start is a Greek letter that means the **universal set**.

ξ = {integers 1 to 10 inclusive}

$A \cap B$ = {1, 9}

$A \cup B$ = {1, 3, 4, 5, 7, 9}

Spinners are used in probability problems and you can find the probability of different events. On this spinner the probability that the spinner doesn't land on green (G) is $\frac{5}{8}$

You can use information given in **tables** to work out probabilities. This table shows the probability of me choosing a particular ice cream! Can you work out the probability that I'll choose toffee?

Flavour	Chocolate	Strawberry	Vanilla	Toffee
Probability	0.2	0.1	0.4	

Key vocabulary

set   probability   venn diagram   universal set   union   intersection

event   outcome   integer   multiple   factor   element

Sets & probability

Date:

Let's remember

1 Estimate £986 - £312

2 Work out mentally 39 × 5

3 Two of the angles in a triangle are 72° and 43°

What is the size of the third angle? $^\circ$

4 Solve $2h + 4 = 10$

$h =$

Let's practise

1

ξ = {integers between 1 and 30 inclusive}

A = {factors of 60}

B = {multiples of 4}

C = {odd multiples of 5}

a) List all the elements in each set.

A _____

B _____

C _____

b) List the elements that are in both set A and C _____

c) Is it possible for any elements to be in both set B and C?
Explain your answer.

_____

_____

2   Students in Year 7 can choose to be involved in any of these after school clubs.

| Drama (D) | Programming (P) | Basketball (B) | Football (F) | Chess (C) |

| Board Games (G) | Knitting (K) | Languages (L) | Ukelele Band (U) |

Mo chooses Basketball, Languages and Ukelele Band.
Rosie chooses Languages, Ukelele Band, Knitting and Football.
Represent this information in the Venn diagram.

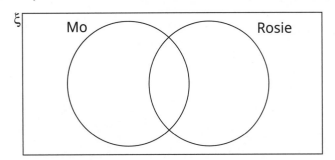

3   100 people completed an online survey about the appliances they use.
The Venn diagram shows some information from the survey.

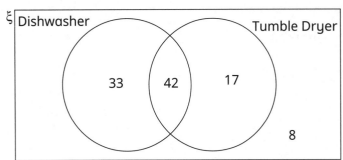

a) How many people use a dishwasher? _____

b) How many people use a tumble dryer? _____

c) How many people use a dishwasher and a tumble dryer? _____

d) How many people use a dishwasher but not a tumble dryer? _____

4   Look at the Venn diagram.

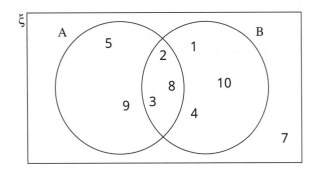

a) Write the elements of $A \cap B$. _____

b) Write the elements of $A \cup B$. _____

5 Tick the sets in which $A \cap B$ would have no elements.

A = {odd numbers}

B = {even numbers}

A = {factors of 10}

B = {multiples of 10}

A = {months with exactly 30 days}

B = {months with exactly 31 days}

6 Draw a possible Venn diagram to represent A and B.

ξ = {integers 1 to 10 inclusive}

$A \cap B$ = {1, 9}

$A \cup B$ = {1, 3, 4, 5, 7, 9}

7 List all the members of each set.

H

ξ = {12, 21, 112, 121, 122, 211, 212, 221}

A = {12, 112, 122, 212}

B = {121, 212}

a) A′ _____

b) B′ _____

c) $A \cap B$ _____

d) $(A \cap B)'$ _____

How did you find these questions?

Very easy   1   2   3   4   5   6   7   8   9   10   Very difficult

Sets & probability

Date:

Let's remember

1 ξ = {integers between 1 and 12}
List the elements of A = {factors of 18}

_____

2 Use the fact that 42 × 31 = 1302 to work out 4.2 × 31 _____

3 Write the angle that is alternate to $\angle MLO$

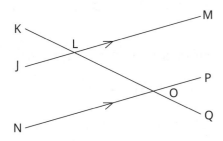

4 $\frac{5}{7} + \frac{1}{3} + \frac{2}{7} + \frac{2}{3} =$ ☐

Let's practise

1 Match each statement to the most appropriate word(s).

It will rain in London every day in April.		impossible
The sun will set in the UK tomorrow.		unlikely
You will roll a 0 on a 6-sided dice.		even chance
You will get a tail when you flip a 50p coin.		likely
It will be sunny in London in August.		certain

2 | B | O | O | K | K | E | E | P | E | R |

The letters are placed into a bag. A letter is chosen at random.

a) Write the sample space for the outcomes. S = {_____}

b) What is the probability that the letter 'R' is selected? _____

c) What is the probability that the letter 'E' is selected? _____

d) What is the probability that a vowel is selected? _____

e) What is the probability that the letter 'W' is selected? _____

3   Kim spins the spinner.
Find the probability of the spinner:

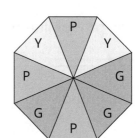

a) landing on purple (P) _____

b) landing on yellow (Y) _____

c) landing on green (G) or yellow (Y) _____

d) not landing on yellow (Y) _____

4   A bag of assorted flavoured chocolates contain 3 toffee, 2 raisin,
4 coffee and 6 orange.
Amir selects a chocolate at random from the bag.
Find the probability that the chocolate selected is:

a) Orange _____

b) Toffee or raisin _____

c) Not coffee _____

5   This box contains some blue and yellow colouring pencils.
Filip removes one of the pencils from the box at random.

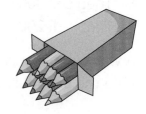

a) On the scale, draw an arrow labelled with a Y to show
the probability that he chose a yellow pencil.

b) On the same scale draw an arrow labelled with a B to
show the probability that he chose a blue pencil.

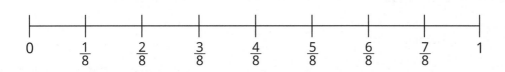

$$0 \quad \frac{1}{8} \quad \frac{2}{8} \quad \frac{3}{8} \quad \frac{4}{8} \quad \frac{5}{8} \quad \frac{6}{8} \quad \frac{7}{8} \quad 1$$

6   A letter card is chosen at random.
Mark on the scale the probability
of getting the letter 't'.

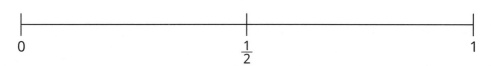

0                          $\frac{1}{2}$ 1

7   Eva is about to choose which flavour of ice cream she would like to eat.
The table shows the probability of Eva choosing each flavour.

Flavour	Chocolate	Strawberry	Vanilla	Toffee
Probability	0.2	0.1	0.4	

a) What is the probability of Eva choosing either chocolate or vanilla?

_____

b) What is the probability of Eva choosing toffee? _____

c) What is the probability of Eva not choosing strawberry? _____

8   The probability that it rains on Sunday is 0.45

What is the probability that it does **not** rain on Sunday? _____

9   Annie plays a game against Dexter in which
   - either of them could win
   - a draw is not possible
   - Annie is twice as likely to win as Dexter.

   What is the probability that Annie wins the game?

   _____

10   A school is running a raffle for charity.
   - They sell 300 blue tickets numbered 1 to 300
   - They sell 200 yellow tickets numbered 1 to 200

A winning ticket is chosen at random.
Find the probability that the ticket selected will be:

a) yellow _____   c) numbered 230 _____

b) numbered 100 _____   d) numbered 500 _____

How did you find these questions?

Very easy   1   2   3   4   5   6   7   8   9   10   Very difficult

Block 5 Prime numbers & proof

In this block you will learn about **prime numbers** and **proof**. **Arrays** can be used to show whether a number is a **factor** of another number. This array shows that 3 is a factor of 24

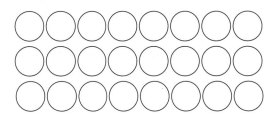

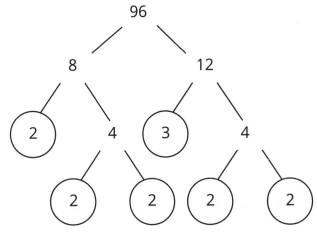

Factor trees can be used to work out to work out all the **prime factors** of any number. Here are the prime factors of 96

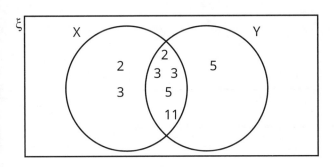

Venn diagrams can be used to show the prime factors of two numbers. This one shows the prime factors of two numbers X and Y. You'll learn how to use it to find the LCM and HCF of the two numbers – that's the **lowest common multiple** and **highest common factor**.

You'll also be exploring **conjectures** and **counterexamples**. Rosie thinks that if you find any multiple of 9 and add its digits together, you'll also get a multiple of 9. Here's an example of where it's true. Do you agree with Rosie?

$$9 \times 58 = 522$$
$$5 + 2 + 2 = 9$$

Key vocabulary

prime number   factor   multiple   common factor

common multiple   prime factor   venn diagram   factor tree   conjecture

counterexample   proof   array   square number   simplest form

triangular number   square number   product

Prime numbers & proof

Date:

Let's remember

1 Write an event that has an even chance of happening.

_____

2 List the elements of set A.
   ξ = {integers between 1 and 8}

   A = {odd numbers}
   B = {numbers less than 5}

_____

3 A pencil sharpener costs 49p.
   Mentally work out the cost of three pencil sharpeners. _____

4 Work out $\frac{7}{15} + \frac{7}{30}$

   Give your answer in its simplest form.

_____

_____

Let's practise

1 Write the first six multiples of each number.

   a) 9   ☐ ☐ ☐ ☐ ☐ ☐

   b) 17 ☐ ☐ ☐ ☐ ☐ ☐

   c) 83 ☐ ☐ ☐ ☐ ☐ ☐

2 a) Draw an array to show that 8 is a factor of 24

  b) Draw an array to show that 3 is not a factor of 10

3 Write a number in each empty box to complete the two-way table.

	Multiple of 8	Not a multiple of 8
Factor of 72		
Not a factor of 72		

4 A number 92 bus leaves the station every 15 minutes between 7 am and 2 pm.
  How many number 92 buses leave the station in a day?

5 Circle the exact number of factors a prime number has.

  0   1   2   4

6 Write down the prime numbers between 30 and 40

  _____

7 Is 27 prime? _____

  Explain how you know.

  _____

  _____

8   Jack says: "Prime numbers are either side of multiples of 6. For example 12 is a multiple of 6, and 11 and 13 are both prime."

a) Give three other examples where Jack is correct.

_____   _____   _____

b) Give an example where Jack is wrong.

_____

9   a) Write down the first 5 square numbers. _____

b) What is the 8th square number?

10   a) Write down the first 5 triangular numbers. _____

b) What is the 8th triangular number?

11   By listing factors of each number, find the highest common factor of 28 and 42

12   Two numbers less than 100 have a highest common factor of 18
What could the two numbers be?
Write down two possible pairs of solutions.

☐ and ☐

☐ and ☐

How did you find these questions?

Very easy   1   2   3   4   5   6   7   8   9   10   Very difficult

Prime numbers & proof

Date:

Let's remember

1. Write the first six multiples of 1.5

   _____

2. A fair six-sided dice is rolled.
   Calculate the probability of the dice landing on a factor of 12

3. If $j + k = 10$, what is the value of $2j + 2k$?

4. Solve $y - \frac{2}{3} = \frac{4}{5}$

   $y =$

Let's practise

1. a) Write the first twelve multiples of 6

   _____

   b) Write the first ten multiples of 9

   _____

   c) Use your lists from parts a) and b) to give common multiples of 6 and 9 which are strictly less than 75

   _____

   d) What is the lowest common multiple (LCM) of 6 and 9?

2. Find the lowest common multiple of each pair of numbers.

   a) 40 and 70   b) 32 and 80

3 Burgers are sold in packs of 8

Buns are sold in packs of 12

What is the least number of packs of burgers and buns you could buy so you have an equal number of burgers and buns?

Packs of burgers ☐   Packs of buns ☐

4 a) Write each of the following numbers as a product of its prime factors.

H

   i) 54   ii) 96

   54 = _____   96 = _____

b) Use a Venn diagram to find the HCF and LCM of 54 and 96

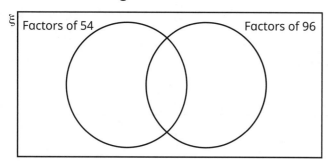

HCF = _____ = ☐

LCM = _____ = ☐

5 Dani works out 510 = 2 × 3 × 5 × 17

Use this information to write these numbers as a product of their prime factors.

a) 1020 = _____   c) 255 = _____

b) 5100 = _____   d) 170 = _____

6 The Venn diagram shows the prime factors of two numbers: X and Y

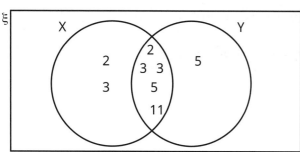

a) Is 55 a common factor of X and Y? _____

b) Write three more common factors of X and Y. ☐ , ☐ , ☐

c) What is the HCF of X and Y?

_____

_____

d) What is the LCM of X and Y?

_____

_____

7 Take any multiple of 3 and add its digits together.
For example 27, 2 + 7 = 9 which is a multiple of 3
Investigate other examples.
Write a conjecture from your findings.

_____

_____

8 Dora conjectures that "the product of two numbers is always greater than each of the numbers".
Find a counterexample to Dora's conjecture.

_____

_____

9 Decide whether each conjecture is always, sometimes or never true.

a) The sum of an odd number and an even number is always odd. _____

b) $a - a = 1$ _____

c) $a + a = a^2$ _____

Time to reflect

Look back through the work you have done this term. Think about what you enjoyed and what you found easy or hard. Talk about this to your teacher and someone at home.

Try these questions	How do you feel about this topic? Tick the box.
Find the value of y $6y$ $2y$ If you need a reminder, look back at the geometric reasoning on pages 98–106	☐ I am confident and could teach someone else. ☐ I think I understand but I need practice. ☐ I don't understand and need help.
Draw a Venn diagram to show these two sets. ξ = {1, 2, 3, 4, 5, 6, 7, 8, 9, 10} A = {even numbers} B = {multiples of 3} If you need a reminder, look back at sets and probability on pages 115–117	☐ I am confident and could teach someone else. ☐ I think I understand but I need practice. ☐ I don't understand and need help.
Here is an array. Which one of these three statements does the array show? ○ ○ ○ ○ ○ ○ ○ ○ ○ ○ ○ ○ ○ ○ ○ ○ ○ a) 6 is a factor of 20 b) 6 is not a factor of 20 c) 20 is a multiple of 6 If you need a reminder, look back at prime numbers on pages 122–127	☐ I am confident and could teach someone else. ☐ I think I understand but I need practice. ☐ I don't understand and need help.